MANIFESTO
Briefing

BY: CRIMINAL PSYCHOLOGIST,
DR. NOMORE DUCKANDCOVER

= BASED ON WHAT'S BEEN STATED IN THIS BOOKLET!
"I AM, THE MOST INTERESTING MAN IN THIS WORLD"...

AuthorHouse™
1663 Liberty Drive
Bloomington, IN 47403
www.authorhouse.com
Phone: 1 (800) 839-8640

Published by AuthorHouse 05/21/2018

ISBN: 978-1-5462-3543-9 (sc)
ISBN: 978-1-5462-3542-2 (e)

♫ *"It's The End Of The World As We Know It"*

'revolution'.
ENOUGH IS ENOUGH!

"Great lessons in protests"

"OVER-ALL, MENTAL HEALTH CARES FINEST HOUR"

Defining mission a must read.

" "PATRIOTISM IS THE BACKBONE OF OUR COUNTRY'
YOURS TRULY, BEST RESTORER OF"

Celebrate America

AMERICAN WRITERS INSTITUTE PROUDLY PRESENTS

JOURNALIST RELEASE OF <u>NEW BOOK ENTITLED</u>

'MANIFESTO
Briefing'

...And They Lived Happily Ever After."

available @ www.authorhouse.com

Phone 1-800-839-8640

"PRESIDENT TRUMP, STRONGLY APPROVED OF 'FAITH
BASED INITIATIVE" - 'SO WATCHA WAITIN FOR?!

FIRST AMENDMENT RIGHT TO READ / FIRST AMENDMENT RIGHT TO PUBLISH...

WANTED

New leader, new nation, new world

'READ <u>HIM</u> AND WEEP'

"My Fellow Americans" **FRIAR FLYER** Discovery Kit

((ANSWERS TO MYSTERIOUS END OF AN AGE PROPHECY FULFILLED))

(((BOOK EXCERPT))) THE P-O-R-P-O-I-S-E OF LIFE —

IS TO SERVE GOD, THRU "HUMAN-KIND" AND `NOT TO BECOME

SHELL-FISH. FACTORY REBORN; I'LL S-E-A YOU AT THE BOOK SIGNING.

=Or= The `Real Day The Earth Stood Still

'MARTIAN PEEPHOLE' DITCH JUNEAU RAT NOW BAYPEE, OLIVE IN WE KNOW, ENVY

= PREFACE =

BIG 'READ' BOOK ANSWERS TO BEING A REALISTIC ROAD MAP TO
'PEACE ON EARTH'. 'MINDFULNESS'
- ASK NOT WHAT 'YOU ASSUME AND OR WANT TO ASSUME, OF GOD'S
EXPECTATIONS OF YOU; 'BUT WHAT GOD'S EXPECTATIONS OF 'YOU
ACTUALLY ARE. - AS YOU WILL FIND IN THIS HERE FORETELLING
BOOK! IN TAKING MY MANIFESTO OUT FOR A TEST DRIVE; 'I LOVE
THE SMELL OF REVOLUTION IN THE MORNING...

= RÈSUMÈ =

I.Q. YOU IN ON THIS!
- LOCATED ON THE BACK COVER DISPLAY
OF THIS HERE BOOK...

(SUB'TITLE)

UNIVERSAL Faith Reformation

Greatest show on Earth campaign!

BIG-TIME INSPIRATION

'RIGHTEOUSLY COMBATING MADNESS'

SUNDAY, NOVEMBER 7, 1999 A Celebration of Faith

Pope challenges to promote Catholicism,

"STATES THAT EVERYONE SHOULD HAVE THE RIGHT TO PROMOTE ONE'S OWN RELIGIOUS BELIEFS!"

NEW WORLD ENTHUSIAM? QUOTE THE ABBREVITED WORDS OF PAKISTANI STUDENT, MALALA YOUSAFZAI!

"ONE TEACHER, ONE BOOK, ONE PEN, CAN CHANGE THE WORLD".

♪ Give'em some of that <u>new</u>-time religion

...And They Lived Happily Ever After."

((CHA--CHING))

"ALWAYS REMEMBER, EVERYTIME A CASH REGISTER BELL RINGS FROM THE PURCHASE OF THIS BOOK, AN ANGEL GETS THEIR WINGS."

DR. SUNDAY Discovery Kit

"THIS HERE BEING A 'END OF DAZE' ON BORROWED TIME CONCLUSION"

Hallelujah! PAGE 3.

((ANSWERS TO MYSTERIOUS END OF AN AGE PROPHECY FULFILLED))

Come on inside!

Celebrate  America

AMERICAN WRITERS INSTITUTE PROUDLY PRESENTS

journalist Release of

MANIFESTO
Briefing
Book That Reveals The Whole Shocking Truth
WHAT YOU NEED TO KNOW
"PLUTOCRACY KILLS"

"THIS THING ABOUT THE LAS VEGAS SHOOTER; 'PROOF THEREOF' IN THE HISTORY OF PEOPLE 'EVER HAVING MEDIA ACCESS; 'NOBODY EVER IMPRESSED HIM ENOUGH TO HAVE CHANGED 'HIS CHOSEN END GAME OF EVENTS MIND". BIG GOT'CHA' - ANSWERS TO:

Atrocities of Democracy. "where to begin"

2012 FAITH FORUM *Do all religions offer a path to God?*

"THE GOOD NEWS MINE DOES 24/7 - 365,. THE BAD - DEMOCRACY DEPRIVED THIS ONE'S BEEN BIG TIME 'ROAD BLOCKED' FOR DECADES.

'THE *GOSPEL ACCORDING* TO PLUTOCRATIC '**Exorcism**'.

best Quote award goes to I.Q. YOU IN ON THIS!!!

"My fellow Americans; the only thing we have to "fear"
is the lack of significant free-speech, or realistic democracy."

OCT. 1ST 2017 **LAS VEGAS** THE SHOOTER: Stephen Paddock,

"RETIRED $$$ WAS A 64-YEAR-OLD WITH A TASTE FOR HIGH-STAKES POKER". 'PULLING STRINGS' AND KNOWING HIS 'STORED UP' FULL BLOWN TEMPER TANTRUM, H-A-T-E FILLED MIND; YOU CAN 'BET' THE DEVIL LEAD HIM INTO 'EVERY CONSISTENT LOOSING SITUATION SO THAT HE COULD FINAL SOLUTION, PULL THIS OFF"...

"Storytelling on a grand scale" PAGE 4.

FUNCTIONALLY HATE DRIVEN CRAZY' IS ONLY HAVING TO 'SHRINK THE HATE PART. ☺

"THY WILL BE DONE ON 'EARTH AS IT IS IN HEAVEN' UNDER NEW MANAGEMENT" YOURS TRULY, 'HEAVEN ON EARTH EDUCATOR' PUTS PERAMBULATING HELL IN PERSPECTIVE, VIA 'SHOW AND TELL' ESSAY

'DETERRENT PROPOSAL'

"I BELIEVE YOU CAN MAKE PEOPLE NICE."

FRIAR FLYER

'THIS WEEK'S SERMON'
'BY THE MONK AMONG YOU'

OCT.31ST
RIGHT
N.Y.C.

'THESIS-CHRIST PEOPLE'

PAGE
5.

DO THE MATH

(2017) COMBINING 'EVERYONES' HEAVY HEART BREAKING $PERSONAL LOSSES$ "ETC". - EVERYTHING FROM THE WAR ZONE HURRICANES, TO THE DEVASTATING CALIF- FIRES; TOSS IN THE LAS VEGAS SHOOTER! - WHO DIDN'T GET TO EXAMINE MY (MEDIA BANNED) 'SHOWSTOPPER' MEMO. THEREFORE, WHAT YOU GOT TO BE ASKING YOURSELVES 'IS WAS, IT ALL $WORTH IT??? 'TO DENIE MY 'LIVE WIRE PRAYERS 'BEING ANSWERED; THUS SENT FORTH FROM GOD'S REVOLUTIONARY, EDUCATIONAL WORD! - OR 'END OF DAZE ON BORROWED TIME!!!

There's no misinterpreting 'Meaning'

FURTHERMORE, PROOF THEREOF' BY WAY OF THESE PURPOSEFUL FONTS DESIGNED BY GOD. - WORKING THRU YOURS TRULY. 'ALWAYS REMEMBER, I'M NOT DOING THIS FOR MY HEALTH AND WELL'BEING, I'M DOING THIS FOR YOU, AND YOURS. WHEREAS TO IGNORE THESE PERIODICALLY SENT FORTH, GOD'S RECHERCHE' EDUCATIONAL WORD, IS NOT TO BE TAKEN LIGHTLY; OR IMPROPERLY DISPOSED OF. 'AS WHY THIS IS WHAT HAPPENED WITH THESE FORETOLD STORIES IN RETROSPECT, 'RESULTING IN' = godZILLA = THE REAL ESTATE = DESTROYER = FILLING IN THE AVAILABLE GAP BY WAY OF CAUSING ALL THIS HORRENDOUS DEATH AND DESTRUCTION. 'ATMOSPHERIC 'POSITIVE (VERSUS) 'ATMOSPHERIC 'NEGATIVE. 'ONLY GOODNESS COMES FROM GOD! 'STARTING OVER WITH YOU, AND YOURS PROTECTION ANYONE??? SIGNED: 'TELL ALL' IN YOUR FACE, CLASS ROOM SAVIOR OF THE WORLD... WHAT'S TRENDING? SCOOP ON OPIOIDS, OR ILLICIT DRUGS! T-SHIRT ANYONE? THE REASON THEY CALL IT 'DOPE' IS THAT NOBODY INTELLIGENT IS TAKING IT. 'SEPARATION FROM REAL AND FAKE'. THEREFORE, 'GET A LIFE, DON'T FORFIT YOURS... IN BRIEF: TALKING POINTS! 'NOSTRIL-DAMUS, PREDICTS THAT THE BEST WAY TO CURB THE 'OVER USAGE OF THE EXPRESSION 'MISERY LOVES COMPANY' IS IN PROVIDING ADEQUATE GLOBAL BIRTH CONTROL...

" When words need to be said "
The Future of earth balance democracy is at stake.
You say you want a revolution?
'THIS IS AMERICA'.

THIS CLASSROOM CONNECTION IS BROUGHT TO YOU BY, 'PEN NAME' DR. SUNDAY, 1980 FOUNDER, OF 'THE POSITIVE FAITH 'ONE WORLD' RELIGION. 'SEEK AND YOU SHALL FIND = THIS HERE BEING A "CRY WOLF" DISCOVERY KIT OF L.M.T. 89503...

LAS VEGAS SHOOTING 10/15/17 (NEWS, UP-DATE)

"ONLY BECAUSE THEY STILL PRETEND THAT THEY HAVEN'T FIGURED OUT A MOTIVE YET"...

'KUDOS TO **RENO GAZETTE-JOURNAL** 10/8/17
PART OF THE USA TODAY NETWORK

'NEWS PRINT' "SPOTLIGHT ON BIG-SPENDING CYCLE"
-AS IF IN SEEING THE FOREST THRU THE TREES.

(TOM PETTY) SONG STATES ♫ EVEN LOSERS GET LUCKY ONCE IN A WHILE!

'RUMER HAS IT THAT HE WON LARGE FORTUNES; AND 'MORE SO' LOST LARGE FORTUNES;
CAUSING HIS NIGHTMARISH SCREAMING IN THE MIDDLE OF THE NIGHT! ♫ KNOW WHEN
TO HOLD'EM -ETC- KNOW WHEN TO RUN.

'MOTIVE OF SHOOTER'

'PAY BACK' -FOR HIS PREDOMINATE GAMBLING LOSSES-
SIMPLY, A HATRED OF PEOPLE THAT KEPT BUILDING FROM HIS COMPOUNDED
GAMBLING FAILURES. 'THUS THE CREATION OF THIS HERE BEING A MONSTER MADE
IN THE U.S.A.

or

I'M SURE HE TOOK TIME OUT FROM HIS 'HATE DRIVEN' BUSY WINNING SCHEDUAL
TO SCOPE OUT CHICAGO AND BOSTON. WHEREBY HE ALWAYS REWARDED HIMSELF AFTER
THESE 'EASY MONEY' GAMBLING WINDFALLS WITH A LUXURIOUS CUISINE AT THE
SENIOR CENTER, RUBBING ELBOWS WITH THE 'LOVE YA BRA' HOMELESS AND SO ON.
WHEREAS MOST LIKELY 60% OF THE ROAD RAGE 'FLIP YOU OFF SOCIETY'
YOU SEE 'IN THIS HERE A GAMBLING TOWN'

"YOU CAN BET"
WAS BY SOMEBODY WHO JUST DROPPED A BUNDLE AT THE CASINO!
- AND THE OTHER 40% IS BY THE POOCH PUNT GUY
WHO'S GIRL'FRIEND JUST LEFT HIM FOR
A 'JOE COCKER SPANIEL...

——— FOR 'ALL THOSE YEARS OF HIS LIFE, BEFORE HE EVER MOVED TO A GAMBLING
COMMUNITY, HE WAS NOTHING MORE THAN A 'YOUR OK, I'M OK' INTROVERTED BORE...
TO MAKE'UM THINK, IS TO MAKE'UM BLINK!

enough to support the brain.

RIGHT FROM WRONG, GOOD FROM EVIL, ON RELIGION? GIVE ME 'ALL YOUR FLUNKIES! YOU DON'T NEED
A WAFER COMMUNION TO BE IN SYNC WITH THIS CRACKER. A MAN HAS GOT TO KNOW 'HIS SAME PAGE
RELIGIOUS LIMITATIONS, OR THE WHOLE WORLD JUST ALL BECOMES A 'GO TO HELL SOCIETY! - AS
LIKE IN ISIS DOGMA, IT'S ALL JUST FOAMING AT THE MOUTH...

TO ALL MY RELIGIOUS COMPETITORS "WHEN YOUR DOGMA QUITS BARKING
FREEDOM OF CHOICE' IS FOR YOU TO PREACH 'MY GOSPEL AND KEEP ALL YOUR
$$$ PARISHIONERS, OR SUFFER THE CONSEQUENCES OF HEAVY DUTY COMPETITION.

THE ADVENTURE
BEGINS HERE

Show and Tell

(1999) SUFFERING FROM INTELLECTUAL GROWTH 'SHUTDOWN; BASED ON DYLAN KLEBOLD'S 'TYPED COLUMBINE COMMENTS STATING - "I KNOW I'M GOING TO A BETTER PLACE THAN HERE". THEREFORE, GIVING HOPE TO FELLOW COPYCATS! "THUS, MY PEN EXPLODED INTO THIS HERE COMBATIVE PAY BACK, ESSAY PRESENTATION"...

"TERRORIST",MASS MURDERERS, SERIAL KILLERS, ETC; 'DETERRENT PROPOSAL' EXAMPLE: ORLANDO, FRANCE, ENGLAND, ETC...

The Horrors of BUSINESS AS USUAL TERRORISM.

"Open Season on Common Folk Citizens"

REMEMBERING those who didn't make it home

'SOMEONE MUST STAND UP TO OUR CLUELESS APOLOGETICAL GOVERNMENT; THEY CAN'T PROTECT US' (VS) THESE WARP MINDED DESPICABLES! THEREFORE, =

WE'RE NOT GONNA TAKE IT ANYMORE BEGINS HERE!

TODAY'S BRIEFING "DETERRENT PROPOSAL"

PROMO EXAMPLE AN 'ALL-FAITHS' mecca FACING WEST

A MULTI-BILLION DOLLAR,'TOURISM PILGRIMAGE'

SATANIC BURIAL GROUND,
'NO PLACE LIKE HELL'
'SPIT ON YOUR GRAVE'
REALISTIC CLOSURE,
HORRIFIC
CRIME,

"DETERRENT PROPOSAL"

"MOCKED FOR ETERNITY"

'YOUR INFAMOUS NAME WRITTEN IN STONE FOR SERVICES RENDERED TO SATAN..

'HELL "IF YOU BUILD THIS THEY WILL COME" HELL'
JUST NORTH OF RENO, NV. OFF 395.
- A FIELD-DAY, DAILY VISITING

'WE WILL OFFICIALLY BURY YOU' PROJECT EXTRAVAGANZA.

'RIGHTEOUSLY COMBATING MADNESS'

" Showstopper becomes 'your call if you want it to be".

essential to formation of a conscience'

WELCOME TO *The United States of Gambling.*

Newsmakers, *A RE-EDITED* 1988 Editorial Democracy Prison Original, **Waiting to Exhale.** 2017, *There's a good chance they're going to recognize him this year,* Announcing **a new** "TRAIN YOUR BRAIN" COURSE OF STRATEGY **ON GAMING UNPREDICTABILITY!** ARTICLES **Refresher Course Revisited.** $ **Games** PEOPLE PLAY

SELF-IMPROVEMENT

Guidelines: *'IN GAMBLING,* **Read, Listen and Win!**

may 1988, **RIPPED FROM THE SKY,** *obey laws of God.*

On Personal Money Management

a 'teachable moment' PAGE 8.

'WINNING A CASINO JACK-POT IS LIKE GETTING A FREE CASH MONEY LOAN THAT VOLUNTARILY SOME PEOPLE WILL PAY BACK WITH ENTRUST.'

'JUST THE FACTS'

"*casinos,* ARE FUN AND EXCITING PLACES OF VENTURE FOR ANY RESPONSIBLE BILL PAYING ADULT, THAT KNOWS THE TRUE VALUE OF WHAT ONE CAN AFFORD TO WAGER' BEFORE MAKING A FOOL OF ONESELF.,

IN THAT EVERYTHING IN LIFE IS TO A DEGREE. WHEREAS THIS IS THE TYPE OF DISCIPLINE ONE MUST ACQUIRE TO *WITHHOLD* **A POSITIVE** Self Esteem ¦:

:WARNING LABEL: 'FOR SOME; LOSING MONEY AT GAMBELING IS PAINFUL, AND CAN MAKE A M-O-N-S-T-E-R OUT OF YOU. "KEEP IN MIND, ALL THOSE PLUSH CASINOS YOU SEE, WERE BUILT ON GAMBLERS LOSINGS"...

"*Spiritual Awakening*" "*cry wolf* discovery kit

Whaddya gonna do America?

"'This Is My Life' Years haven't been kind. words surely can change meanings; 'join protest' STACK PAGES HAVE IT ALL !

"OPEN SEASON ON COMMON FOLK CITIZENS"

THIS IS WHAT CON-SOUL-ING 'THOUGHTS AND PRAYERS' LOOK LIKE ON PAPER.
SIGNED: CRIMINAL PSYCHOLOGIST, DR. NOMORE DUCKANDCOVER

HISTORY ON DISPLAY ANALYSIS 6/16

Religious 'extremists'. Or 'REALISTIC POSSIBILITY ABOUT =FREQUENT FLYER=

'ORLANDO NIGHTCLUB GUNMAN'S PRIORITIZED MOTIVE?!

I BELIEVE THE 'REAL STORY' BEHIND THE STORY' WAS THAT
'THIS' WAS A 'GAY GUY' MISFIT WITH A MONSTER PERSONALITY;

THAT COULDN'T FIND ANYBODY WANTING TO DANCE SHEIK

TO SHEIK WITH HIM. FRUSTRATED AND HAVING AN EFFETE FEELING
OF BEING A MATEENE WIENIE WITHIN THE 'IN CROWD'. 'SEXUALLY
UN-FULFILLED HE REVENGEFULLY TOOK OUT ALL OF HIS FRUSTRATIONS
OUT ON THE CLUB'S PATRONS!

Americans wonder: Where can I be safe?

IS NIGHTCLUB MASSACRE KILLING THE NEW NORM; ALONG WITH A JIHADI
DRIVERS ED; CRASH COURSE IN USING REAL DUMMIES WITH A 'INVALID'
LICENSE TO KILL??? **Vintage Journalism**; "END OF DAZE ON BORROWED TIME; 'POLICE
STATE" THAT EVERYTIME 'POSITIVE SUGGESTMENT GET'S TOSSED OUT
"SUCH AS IN THIS HERE **ETC**' * NEGATIVITY. WILL ALWAYS BE THERE TO
FILL IN THE GAP * IN BRIEF: HOW TO SAY SOMETHING IN SO MANY WORDS!!!

MAY--DAY **Time to Rescue** RELIGION; *Humans need to evolve*.

"ALL THIS 'HAS GOT TO BECOME' YESTERDAYS PRAYER BOOK!!!"
((("WHAT STARTED WITH RELIGION CAN ONLY BE RECTIFIED BY RELIGION".)))

NEWS OF RECORD on **NATIONWIDE Gunman** GONE WILD,

THE GOSPEL ACCORDING TO A *Call Time Out!*

Someone must stand up to our government

CONNECTICUT SCHOOL MASSACRE DECEMBER 14, 2012 "President Obama,
What we have not seen is leadership: not from the White House and not from Congress.
That must end today. This is a national tragedy and it demands a national response."

Heard Any Good 'SHOW STOPPER' Sermons Lately?

TAKING AWAY ONE'S EVIL EXCUSES, 'BREAK ON THRU TO THE OTHERSIDE'
moral revolutionary FOCUS BE **On** NOWHERE TO 'MR. HYDE' === BY DR. JEKYLL!
'LEAD US NOT INTO TEMPATION; BUT DELIVER US FROM "EVER BECOMING EVIL" AMEN...
'ELEMENTARY MY DEAR 'WHAT-SON? 'YOU GOT A SURE LOCK
ON THIS 'ALL GOD'S CHILDREN' CASE CONSTABLE...

= *this here being a "cry wolf" discovery kit of L.M.T. 89503*

IMPORTANT NOTICE

"OPEN SEASON ON COMMON FOLK CITIZENS"

" The Shots Still Echo "

Gunman fired point-blank at crying children in church,

HISTORY ON DISPLAY.

" Vegas shooter had lost money "

❚ FROM THE 'GET GO' EXACTLY WHAT 'I WROTE AND SAID ABOUT! - TOSS IN SHOWSTOPPER 'MEMO, PLUS GAMBLERS PRAYER ESSAY; WITH THIS HERE PROMO STORY FOR A KICKER."

'showcases the truth about what's happening behind the scenes 'WITH

A teachable moment' wake-up call Exhibit

CLOCK IS TICKING ON

'THIS THING IS NOT OVER'.

Honoring Divine Inspiration ANYONE ?

The
POSITIVE
SPIRIT
long reach:

HOLY 'Ghost Stories' Word Power:

'SYNCHRONIZING OUR MORAL COMPASS'

'revolutionary crunch time' Or

Same Old story different day !

Imagemakers "stop this cover-up."

"WHAT WE HAVE 'HERE IS A FAILURE TO COMMUNICATE"

" The Gospel according to If you Build This "

⊙ne f⊙r the b⊙⊙ks
"TEACHING INTELLIGENCE"
Review of reviews:

IN QUESTION THE CASE OF S.CAROLINA, CHURCH MASS MURDERER,'DYLANN ROOF' "ETC".
LACKING "THIS" EDUCATION, HE WAS A '<u>UN-CHALLENGED</u>'
FREE-RANGE NARROW MINDED RACIST...

— A MORALIST APPROACH TO EDUCATION! THEREFORE, H-A-T-E
C-R-I-M-E 'NEGATIVE SPIRIT BUSTING, PRESENTED BY YOURS TRULY!

THIS HERE PRIOR 'VINTAGE JOURNALISM SHOWSTOPPER' WAS A -

'NATIONWIDE LETTERS TO THE EDITOR' ETC,
"FAITH BASED INITIATIVE, MEDIA BANNED,
WE THE PEOPLE COVer up. <u>Atrocities of Democracy.</u>

"THE WORDS 'SEPERATION
OF CHURCH AND STATE'
ARE NOT FOUND
IN THE CONSTITUTION"

"FREEDOM OF EXPRESSION REFERS NOT JUST TO THE
MEDIA BUT ALSO TO THE FREEDOM OF ALL CITIZENS'
FREEDOM TO THINK, SPEAK, WRITE AND EXPRESS
THEMSELVES WITHOUT GOVERMENT RETALIATION. IT
PROTECTS THE RIGHT OF 'MINORITIES TO BE HEARD
AND PROMOTES CREATIVITY, OF NEW IDEAS AND
SOLUTIONS THAT CAN BENEFIT THE NATION".

BACK-TO-SCHOOL WITH 'LITERARY' RACIST <u>EXORCISM</u> CLASS 101 ••• PAGE 11.

"THE
PRIORITY OF EDUCATION' IS THAT OF BEING A MORAL ONE". (VERSUS) STATUS QUO ED.

When words need to be said   COMMON CORE PROPOSAL

TEACHING INTELLIGENCE, "SPOTLIGHT ON RACISM"

THE CLEAR THINKING COMMON GROUND OF <u>ONE</u>'S <u>HAVING</u>
<u>INTELLIGENCE, IS SITUATIONALLY BEING ABLE TO</u>
<u>ACKNOWLEDGE, OR DETECT</u> --- <u>EXAMPLE:</u> GOOD COP, BAD COP;
GOOD WHITE MAN, BAD WHITE MAN; GOOD BLACK MAN, BAD BLACK MAN;
GOOD PIT-BULL, BAD PIT-BULL; <u>ETC</u>, <u>ETC</u>, <u>ETC</u>. A TEACHABLE MOMENT?
WHEREAS 'THICK-SKINNED' ETERNAL OPTIMISM, IS HOW ONE FINISHES
FIRST IN THE HUMAN RACE. SIGNED: DR.SUNDAY, HOORAY FOR OUR SIDE..
= IN TESTIMONY WHEREOF = THIS IS ONE'S 'POSITIVE' BRAIN ON REPEAT DIALING!
WHEREAS TO FIND 'POSITIVE SAMENESS' WITHIN YOUR FELLOW MAN 'IS TO FIND HEAVEN
ON EARTH' S-A-N-E-N-E-S-S = AMEN.
• SO HERE'S LOOKING AT YOU KID! THE FORMULA TO ONE'S OVER-ALL
LIKABILITY AND ACCEPTANCE IS WHAT'S AT STAKE HERE.

CONCLUSIVELY: ANTISEMITIC ETC; FLORIDA SCHOOL SHOOTER, WAS JUST ANOTHER
EDUCATIONALLY <u>UN-CHALLENGED</u> FREE-RANGE WIND-UP DOLL!!! PRE-MENTAL HEALTH
PREVENTION CLINIC; WAS WRITTEN BY SOMEONE WHO WAS SMART ENOUGH TO...
THE PURSUIT OF HAPPINESS IS NOTHING BUT A CON --- STITUTION.

imagemakers Set my news free.
The truth about mass shootings PAGE 12.

!

— BE NICE FOR 'CHRIST SAKE' WASN'T WORKING FOR **THEM** ——!

"My Fellow Americans; The art of restoring magnetic heads
CRITICAL THINKERS (READ) **what you've been missing**

exemplifies What you need to know **AND** Process.

News, notes, quips & quotes

Observations, confessions and revelations

'essential to formation of a conscience

Discover a New Dimension in Learning

"QUOTE" (ZEPPELIN SONG) ♫ I REALLY WANT TO KNOW; HOW MUCH THERE IS TO KNOW ?

"GREAT BIBLICAL INTERPRETATIONS"

GETTING IT RIGHT.

ALL CONTRIBUTING TO A **contagious -philosophy**

REVITALIZING NEW—AGE 'SET YOU STRAIGHT' CURRICULUM ANYONE?

"CHALLENGING THE 'WE KNOW EXACTLY HOW YOU WERE THINKING' MIND'SET
OF THE LAS VEGAS, AND TEXAS, EVILDOERS ETC, WITH"

THE 'NEGATIVE SPIRIT DWELLING' SELF-CENTERED 'MIND'
IS THE DEVIL'S (WORKSHOP)!!! # HASH TAG, SNAP OUT
OF IT. — TRANSFIGURATIVELY — NOWHERE TO MR.HYDE'

This is not your father's religion •

PSYCHOLOGY ON ORDER:
((("COMMON DENOMINATOR")))

"WHEREAS TO KNOW ONE'S WORKABLE MIND, IS TO
BLOW ONE'S MIND; TILL THEY GET YOURS TRULY, 'TRUTH
SERUM MENTALLY OVERHAULED, NOTHINGS GOING TO CHANGE.
IMMUNE TO UN—IMPACTIVE NEANDERTHAL RELIGIONS DILLY,
DALLY, DOGMA! 'EVIL MINDED CLOSET ATHEISTS' ARE
NOTHING MORE THAN 'FREE-RANGE' REAL LIFE FOCUSED
ZOMBIES ON A MISSION FROM godZILLA · · ·

WHO AM I? SIGNED: YOURS TRULY, IN CASTING OUT DEVIL'S'

I'M THE DEVIL'S WORST NIGHTMARE!!!

= FRIAR FLYER=

"Open Season on Common Folk Citizens"

REMEMBERING **those who didn't make it home**

HISTORY ON DISPLAY

NEWS OF RECORD on **NATIONWIDE Gunman** GONE WILD,

Americans wonder: Where can I be safe?

Someone must stand up to our government

Resistance must be heard PAGE 13.

"WHAT WE HAVE 'HERE IS A FAILURE TO COMMUNICATE".

'PARKLAND FLORIDA, "ETC" ST.VALENTINE'S DAY MASSACRE!!!
"EVIL END GAME, SHOWSTOPPER DETERRENT PROPOSALS; A 'IN
YOUR FACE' BREAK'THROUGH" ((ENOUGH IS ENOUGH)) ANSWERS TO
THIS HERE BEING A "CRY WOLF" DISCOVERY KIT OF L.M.T. 89503
"My fellow Americans; WORDS ARE THE BEST WEAPON! - AND I NEED YOUR WRITTEN
AND OR VERBAL, HOUNDING OF THE MEDIA ETC; THUS BETTER LIVING THRU DISCOVERY. **"**

"IF YOU BUILD THIS THEY WILL COME"
'OR'

- JUST ANOTHER WALK IN THE PARK OF 'END OF DAZE ON
BORROWED TIME' FEATHER RUFFLING, 'BUSINESS AS USUAL ?

FLO.TEX.VEGAS,ETC! **"THE SHOOTER:** 'THESIS CHRIST PEOPLE!
'PROOF THEREOF' IN THE HISTORY OF
PEOPLE 'EVER HAVING MEDIA ACCESS; 'NOBODY EVER IMPRESSED HIM ENOUGH TO HAVE
CHANGED 'HIS CHOSEN END GAME OF EVENTS MIND".
=MENTAL=HEALTH=CARE=

WELCOME TO *The* formation of a conscience

by A UNIQUE SOURCE of SUPERIOR WISDOM...

"IN BRIEF" 'HOW TO SAY SOMETHING IN SO MANY WORDS.

1999 VINTAGE JOURNALISM; 'A ON GOING FAITH BASED INITIATIVE'
COVER-UP CONSPIRACY! WHEREAS WITHOUT' YOURS TRULY PROPOSED SET
OF CONSEQUENCES 'THERE'S NO SECOND THOUGHTS TO ONE'S EVER DOING
THESE EVIL DESPICABLE DEEDS; - SO - MUCH - SO THAT IT 'COULD VERY
WELL CHANGE THEIR FUNCTIONALLY MOTIVATED 'MIND' FROM EVER RESPONDING TO
THESE HERE SCRIPTED 'ACTS' IN THE FIRST PLACE! SIGNED: PROGRAMER.

GEE; WITH ALL THESE MUCH NEEDED HOLD YOUR GROUND DINOSAUR KILLING,
ASSAULT WEAPONS; - THEY'VE BEEN WORKING ON IMPROVING BACKROUND CHECKS
FOR THE PAST 20, YEARS. - WHEN THIS SHOULD HAVE ALL BEEN PROFECTED/
WITHIN THE FIRST YEAR. 'AMEN... HOW DO YOU LIKE ME NOW???
OUTTA THIS WORLD AND ON WITH THE NEXT?! WHO AM I? METAPHORICALLY
SPEAKING! "I'M YOUR NEW WORLD ADAM"...

'WORDS ARE THE BEST WEAPONS'
AND IT'S THIS KIND OF AMMO,
THAT'LL KEEP PEOPLE
IN LOCK STEP.
'A HOW TO 'COMBAT P.T.S.D GUIDE'
- AT YOUR SERVICE...

Discover a New Dimension in Learning

GETTING IT RIGHT. PAGE 14.

Observations, revelations,

News, notes, quips & quotes

ALL CONTRIBUTING TO A **contagious-philosophy**

exemplifies What you need to know **AND** Process.

'ANALYSIS OF KNOWING RIGHT FROM WONG'

- HE HAD THE FUNCTIONAL ABILITY TO DRIVE OVER TO THAT VA FACILITY,
AND STOP FOR EVERY STOP LIGHT; THUS GET THERE WITHOUT INCIDENT;
AND WHAT THAT TELLS ME IS THAT 'HE WAS MENTALLY WORKABLE; AND WAS
'NEVER GIVEN MY DECADES OLD MEDIA BANNED 'MEMO' TO DRAW TO A CHA-
LLENGING CONCLUSION 'ABOUT HAVING A PURPOSE IN LIFE; AS WRITTEN BY
YOURS TRULY. - CALLED 'PRAYER OF A SANE MAN'. - ARE YOU AWARE THAT
IN THE 'BIG PICTURE OF LIFE; ONLY A 'TRUE PREDOMINANTLY 'POSITIVE
SPIRIT FILLED' GOD LOVING PROGRAMED PERSON, WOULD ONLY KILL IN SELF
-DEFENSE, WAR, OR JUSTIFIABLE CAPITAL PUNISHMENT? FURTHERMORE, THOU
SHELT NOT 'INSTIGATE KILL! STEAD'FAST WITH THIS HERE EVOLUTIONARY,
REVOLUTIONARY, THOUGHT PROCESSING SHOWSTOPPER! - THE 'NEGATIVE SP-
IRIT DWELLING' SELF-CENTERED 'MIND' IS (THE DEVIL'S WORKSHOP) ###

HASH TAG - SNAP OUT OF IT!!! TRANSFIGURATIVELY, NOWHERE TO 'MR. HYDE'.
(EXAMPLE) 'A P.T.S.D NIGHTMARE SWITCH AND BATE REMEDY? - LISTEN TO
MUSIC A GOOD PORTION OF THE DAY, AND OR NIGHT, AND CHANCES ARE ONE
OF THOSE CATCHY SONGS YOU LIKE OR NOT, HAUNTINGLY WILL 'BRAIN WORM'
BE PLAYING OVER AND OVER AGAIN IN YOUR HEAD AS YOU SLEEP; AS OPPOSED
TO THE CONTRARY. (EXAMPLE) - AS LIKE WHAT I WROTE ABOUT SNIPER KYLE,
IN TWITTER - HE SHOULD HAVE TAKEN HIS KILLER TO DISNEYLAND "ETC" AS
OPPOSED TO P.T.S.D LAND. 'OR (EXAMPLE) WATCH FREQUENTLY 2 HRS, OF OLD
SCHOOL 3 STOOGES FILMS, AT NIGHT BEFORE YOU GO TO BED; AND YOU'LL
WAKE UP IN THE MORNING WANTING TO BECOME A ROCKET SCIENTIST. WHERE-
AS, IT'S 'HOW ONE' KEEPS P.T.S.D ON A 'NEVER ADVANCING BACK BURNER.
FURTHERMORE, SHOULD YOU SUGGEST THE 'RESPONSIBILITY OF PET ADOPTION - PRICELESS.

THE SEARCH FOR SIGNS OF INTELLIGENT LIFE IN THE UNIVERSE?

'THIS HERE BEING A NATIONWIDE COAST TO COAST, PLUTOCRATIC SOLIDAR-
ITY, MELT'DOWN DISCOVERY KIT OF YOURS TRULY, VIA SEEK AND YOU SHALL
FIND AUTHOR, L.M.T 89503, THUS WELCOME TO WE KNOW... MARCH2018

Man in video cites rejection, blames women
Calif. murder suspect had manifesto of rampage

"I didn't want it to come to this," Rodger said. "I desperately wanted a way out."

"QUOTE NEWS PRINT HEAD-LINE SET-UP"/ WITH STORY RESPONSE FOLLOW-UP BY YOURS TRULY.
(SEXUAL HEALING) "WELCOME TO THE 'END' OF SWEEPING HUMAN SEXUALITY UNDER
THE RUG" • 'RX' WHEREBY THIS HERE BEING 'SHOCK THERAPY' TO THE SO-CALLED
GOODY TWO SHOES IMAGE CONSCIOUS, NATIONWIDE STRAIT JACKET ASSOCIATION, ETC. ETC.

KNIVES, AND GUNS, AND A VEHICLE, OH' MY; THIS GUY RODGER
SHOULD HAVE BEEN 'LITERALLY DIAGNOSED AS ONE HORNY DEVIL!
BY WAY OF HIS CRYING OUT FOR HELP VIDEO AND MANIFESTO, IS
ALL EVIDENCE TO THAT. THEREFORE, ENTER YOURS TRULY, HISTOR
-ICALLY THE MOST GIFTED SHRINK THAT'S EVER WRITTEN A 'RX'.
ALL HE NEEDED TO DO TO RECYCLE HIS MINDSET AND FUNCTION
NORMALLY, WAS TO HAVE SPENT THAT WEEKEND AT A'WHORE HOUSE;
AND BY MONDAY EVENING THE NEW MISTER DYNAMIC PERSONALITY,
WOULD HAVE PROBABLY BEEN OUT DOING STAND -UP COMEDY!

"INTRODUCING 'COUGAR CITY' EPOCHAL PROPOSAL"

♫ MONEY AIN'T FOR NOTHING, AND THE COUGARS ARE ALL FREE.

'WHERE BOY MEETS PEARL' WHEREBY ONE WOMENS TRASH, IS ANOTHER WOMENS TREASURE!
50 SHADES OF BEING OVER 50, TO A COUGAR; GUYS IN THEIR 20'S ARE PRICELESS.

'IF YOU BUILD THIS THEY WILL COME'•

Time to reach the next level of

HARMONY? - "I'D EVEN GO AS FAR AS HAVING A $20 DOLLAR,
PLAIN JANE, HORNY WOMENS WHORE HOUSE; THUS ACTION FOR EVERYBODY HORNY.

'Time has come' for Invention of the Year

"LEGALIZE 'CONSENTING' NO STRINGS ATTACHED PROSTITUTION" ESPECIALLY
IN THE ='VACINITY'= OF COLLEGE AND MILITARY INSTATUTIONS., WITH ALL THE
THANK YOU FOR YOUR SERVICE, OPEN SEASON' MILITARY MALE SEX OFFENDERS OUT
THERE, ALONG WITH ALL THE 'INTOLORABLE' ONE IN FIVE COLLEGE YOUNG WOMEN
BEING SEXUALLY ASSULTED!!! YEARS AGO I SENT THIS SAME INFO,
OUT TO THE NATIONWIDE MEDIA AND THEY NEVER WROTE BACK TO
THANK ME! IN REGARDS TO THIS CLONE CREEP, STORY OF
CHO-SEUNG-HUE KILL 32! HUE, WAS A HORNY DEVIL 'R-E-J-E-C-T'
REVENGEFUL EVIL DOER FROM A PICK AND CHOOSE ESCORT SERVICE
DENYING HIM SERVICE, AND THE REST IS ALL HISTORY. IN
CONCERT WITH REVENGE, OR SUFFERING FROM BROKEN HEART SYNDROM,
JOKER HOLMS, WAS IN NEED OF SET YOU STRAIGHT 'RX' SEXUAL THERAPY•

READY FOR PRIME TIME
Church of Open Door MINISTER

DOCTOR OF RELIGIOUS SCIENCE **Dr. Sunday** A HEAVEN ON EARTH EDUCATOR.

GETTING TO KNOW **DR.Sunday** 'BY WAY OF SOME OF HIS TWEETS! ☞

Writer's on the storm !

☞ (VERSUS) THE INCUMBENT NEANDERTHAL RELIGION; 'DEUTERONOMY' IS NOW

-DUDE-WILL-RAT-ON-ME !

IN REFERENCE TO 'LGBT' DISCRIMINATORY PRACTICES...

"People should not be discriminated against."

☞ (((GRANDFATHERD' IN; THUS USING 'CAPS FOR LIFE; BY WAY OF MY CLASSIC 'MAY-DAY' ESSAYS BEING SENTENCED TO A LIFE IN DEMOCRACY PRISON VIA THE 'WAR OF THE COLD SHOULDER!!!)))

☞ POSITIVE STIMULUS; LET 'MUSIC BECOME 'YOUR DRUG OF CHOICE!!! ♫

☞ P.S. AUTHOR <u>YOURS TRULY, POLITICALLY</u> SPEAKING, <u>IS A</u> NO WOODEN NICKLES TAKING CONSERVATIVE, HEART OF GOLD PROGRESSIVE '<u>LIBERTARIAN</u>'.

R.G.J 'FAITH FORUM'

Does God have a sexual gender?

(SCRIPTURE'S FINEST HOUR)

"TRUTH IS STRANGER THAN FICTION"

Own A Moment In Time

' STORYBOOK ON THE ORIGINAL SIN;

PROMOTION OF TOP BILLING 'GENDER' MAN-IPULATION .

'GLOBALLY SPEAKING; HISTORICALLY, 'FOR THE MOST PART WOMEN' HAVE BEEN BACK SEAT JERKED AROUND FOR ATLEAST A COUPLE OF WEEKS NOW !!!

And best Quote award goes to PAGE 15.

"HISTORY, HAS ALWAYS BEEN - HIS - STORY"...

Spiritual Awakening message A wake-up call Exhibit 'Life' according to (**New-age**) **Catechism Lessons**
"Higher Truths"

TIMES ARE A CHANGIN'

Should you study other religions before adopting one?
Writer traces roots of religion

"FOR WHAT STARTED WITH 'RELIGION, CAN ONLY BE 'RECTIFIED BY RELIGION!!!"

"IN BRIEF: *Life according to* **a new modern**
DAY <u>RELIGIOUS</u> CLEAN SLATE."

exemplifies What you needed to know **AND** Process.

Life Lessons as Timeless as Infinity

'ALWAYS WAS AND ALWAYS WILL BE' GOD Holy Spirit' (EOE) is The **Positive Spirit** = without gender.

1980 *foundation of God's new world* by **Dr. Sunday**.

<u>INFORMATION</u> BANK: GOD is <u>THE</u>.
The Positive <u>SPIRIT</u> Without <u>GENDER</u>.

"ALL GOD'S CHILDREN, HISTORIC INAUGURAL DECLARATION"

'WORD ON' LEGENDARY MAVERICK 'PREACHER YOURS TRULY, "SANITY CLAUSE"

"for I am no better than any human –kind person – in any human-kind situation "

= Speaks volumes.) WALK IN MY SHOES P-L-E-A-S-E.

THE Positive spirit, **PRESCRIPTION STRENGTH**

WITHIN, **Sheds Light on the Body of the Beholder!**.

PROPITIOUSLY AN EQUAL OPPERTUNITY EMPLOYER.

'All God's children Apostle Lips Now.' *'If you see something <u>here</u> say something!*

ALL BIRDS OF A FEATHER CREATED EMOTIONALLY EQUAL

Today's, Briefing *Teaching Intelligence, "Spotlight on Racism"*

Blessed are the "true" Lovers of God; for within this interactive prayer rapport with God, racism doesn't exist!

"Therefore to find 'positive sameness' within your fellow man 'is to find S-A-N-E-N-E-S-S = Amen

THE P-O-R-P-O-I-S-E OF LIFE IS TO SERVE GOD, THRU "HUMAN-KIND" AND

NOT TO BECOME SHELL-FISH • FACTORY REBORN; I'LL S-E-A YOU AT THE BOOK SIGNING...

♫ AMERICA, AMERICA, GOD SHED ~~HIS~~ THY GRACE ON ME!!!

"Storytelling on a grand scale"
THE POSITIVE Faith Religion

Laying Claim to Ministry of Higher Education ...
PAGE 16.

IN GOD WE TRUST

- WHO'S THE BEST 'REANIMATE SALES PERSON,
TEACHER SPOKESPERSON, FOR GOD?
'YOURS TRULY, AT YOUR
SERVICE!

'IN BRIEF
EXAMPLE' 'RELIGIOUSLY SPEAKING, WHAT WE HAVE HERE IS A HISTORIC
FAILURE TO RATIONALIZE. THEREFORE, A 'RE-REASONING RELOAD,
STARTING WITH THE FIRST AND FOREMOST COMMANDMENT! "I AM 'THE
LORD THY GOD, THOU SHELT 'NOT HAVE 'ANY FALSE 'gods'BEFORE ME".
OR 'CLOSE ENOUGH FOR RELIGIOUS WORK'. 'INTELLECTUALLY SPEAKING,
'HISTORICALLY SPEAKING, "NOBODY ABSORBED THE MEMO"...

(REVISITED EXAMPLES.) HISTORY 1927, START OF WORK ON THE DON'T
TRY TO CON---GOD THE POSITIVE SPIRIT, = ABOUT YOUR <u>FALSE god CREATION</u>
CELEBRATION <u>OF MT. RUSHMORE, THUS GOLDEN FLEECE,</u> INTHAT SAY CHEESE 'GOD
ONLY PICTURED US HERE! RESULTING IN THE 1929 STOCK MARKET CRASH, ALONG WITH
30'S DUST BOWL AND DEPRESSION; LEADING ALL THE WAY UP TO THE 1941, COMPLETION
OF MT. RUSHMORE, AND THE WELCOMING INTO WWII, OR 'HELL ON EARTH PERSONIFIED.
UPGRADED FROM THE REST OF US SLOBS, PRIOR TO THE HOLOCAST; THE JEWISH PEOPLE
WERE ONCE REFERRED TO AS THE CHOSEN PEOPLE; AND DEMON POSSESSED HITLER,
ACCOMMODATED. RECONFIRMING ALL GOD'S CHILDREN. August 2005 *HURRICANE KATRINA
CREATIVE CURRENTS! BLAME IT ON THE 'RIO FALSE GOD SON WORLD, WORSHIP EXHIBIT.*

'GOLDEN FLEECE REVISITED,

REFLECTIVELY, HOW ABOUT THE EASTER ISLAND 'FALSE GOD,
STATUE CREATION STORY, OF ALL THOSE PEOPLE THAT VANISHED ●

What you need to know

YOU CAN'T TOSS 'THE' BOSS FOR A LOSS.
'ONLY GOODNESS COMES FROM GOD'.

"**GOD**, HOLY SPIRIT IS A CONSTANT; PURE LOVE'S ONE AND ONLY
SENDER, 'THE POSITIVE SPIRIT WITHOUT GENDER. IN ACCORDANCE
WITH - TO LITERALLY PUSH GOD'S SPIRITUAL MESSAGE AWAY! - AN
EVIL LURKING godZILLA, FILLING IN THE GAP WILL ALWAYS BE THERE
TO ACCOMODATE YOU. **WAKE UP AND SMELL THE BARRAGE OF ON GOING DEMONIC
DISASTERS THAT HAVE BEEN TAKING PLACE!** A ATMOSPHERIC WEATHER PREVAILING
<u>DEVASTATION</u> ●

INVESTIGATING THE ON GOING <u>SPIRITUAL BATTLE</u> GAME
OF POSITIVE 'RAIN, **(versus)** NEGATIVE 'RAIN, EXAMPLE ETC.

ELEMENTS OF POSITIVITY VS. ELEMENTS OF NEGATIVITY! NEGATIVE COMPONENTS
OF HIGH WINDS, DRY CONDITIONS CONDUCIVE TO ALL THOSE CALIFORNIA FIRES...

ATMOSPHERIC POSITIVE SPIRIT. ((VERSUS)). ATMOSPHERIC NEGATIVE SPIRIT

'Life' *according to* A LARGE SCALE WEATHER PREVAILING ENVIRONMENT.   ARMAGEDDON
TO YOU YET!?

THE SEARCH FOR SIGNS OF INTELLIGENT LIFE IN THE UNIVERSE?

"WELCOME TO THE ROCKET SCIENCE GRADUATE SCHOOL OF READING AND
COMPREHENSION! YOURS TRULY, THE ROCKET SCIENTOLOGIST THAT'S
GONE FATHER, OR A' FURTHER, THAN ANY FLESH AND BLOOD MAN".

Nevada's hidden gem revealed

On record 2001 YOURS TRULY (SHOW) PROPOSAL

(((SERMON CITY CATHEDRAL)))

SERMON CITY, <u>PROJECT PROPOSAL</u> TO BECOMING
RENO'S `BEST OVER—ALL TOURIST ATTRACTION!!!

'TOSS IN THA NEVADA CEMETERY, EVILDOER PROJECT PROPOSAL'

★ Dr.Sunday show

'AN ALL GOD'S CHILDREN ACCEPT ALL'
TELEVISION MINISTRY *TAPE* Live from Reno

"STATEMENT 'SEPERATION OF CHURCH AND STATE' IS NOT FOUND IN THA CONSTITUTION".

A different kind of church discover where you fit in

PLAN ON RECORD-BREAKING TELEVISION.

*WHAT'S IN STORE? WATCH HIM RISE FROM THA DEAD,
MASSIVE AUDIENCES OF* 'BORED AGAIN CHRISTIANS' *THAT WERE
BORED TO DEATH, WITH STATEMENTS LIKE 'IF I'M
VIRTUALLY HONEST ENOUGH TONIGHT, I SHOULD BE
ABLE TO END FREEDOM OF SPEACH!'* NOTE:'THA=MAN,'THE=GOD...

THE GOSPEL ACCORDING TO RELIGION & POLITICS

A PRODUCT OF A **SUPERCONNECTED** MAN, AND HIS **GOD**.

Time to Rescue *tha* NEANDERTHAL DISCRIMINATORY *Once Upon A Time Bible'* ETC,ETC.

A work of monumental religious and political significance.

FOR 'ALL' INSPIRATIONAL AND INGENIOUS PROPHETS; <u>WILL BE UPDATED AND ETERNALLY OPEN;</u>
REWRITTEN FOR THA PEOPLE OF OUR TIMES, AND ALL TIMES'...

'FORMULA TO PROPHECY DECLARED DEAD AWAKEN TO A NEW LIFE. SIGNED: *THA COMMISSIONER*

programs promote variety

DON'T UNDERESTIMATE PAGE 18.

Get ready for fantastic shows. *PROGRAMING:*

What's Up Doc? PODIUM SEGMENT. WEEKLY NEWS & REVIEW,
ACCORDING TO AUTHOR'S CREDENTIALS. ((COMEDY SEGMENT.))
TRUCK LOADS OF YOURS TRULY WRITTEN SKITS, ACTING WITH GUEST.
((FATHER THYME, COOKING SEGMENT.)) OVER—ALL SPECIALTY COOKING
ALONG WITH OPEN HOUSE CONTEST BY YOURS TRULY, WITH GUEST.
((MUSIC SEGMENT.)) = AN OCCASIONAL BRING DOWN THA HOUSE
AND SENATE, ROCK 'N ROLL = BLUES SINGING 'BY YOURS TRULY.

story REFLECTION Meter Is Running.

Friends for life

CBS NEWS PROMO CONTEST, 'NOTE TO SELF'!
'RECOGNITION TO THOSE'
'BLESSED ARE ALL THE POSITIVE PLUS,
$CHARITABLE GIVERS OF THIS WORLD;
WITH ALL THE EXAMPLES OF 'GOOD DEED
DOING' HEARTFELT VOLUNTEERS, IN THIS
HERE A GLOBAL SOCIETY MAKING THIS WORLD
A MORE BEARABLE PLACE TO LIVE. - ALONG
WITH THE LIKES OF DOCTORS WITHOUT BOARDERS,
'HABITAT FOR HUMANITY' "ETC" 'RIGHT ON THRU
TO ALL THE PERSON OR PERSONS, THAT WOULD
GIVE YOU THE SHIRT, OR SHIRTS OFF THEIR BACKS!
SIGNED: BEACH BUMS ANONYMOUS. :)

TIMES ARE A CHANGIN'

APRIL/2018

Licensed to work

RÉSUMÉ FOLLOW-UP: YOURS TRULY,

A G.I. BILL PSYCHOLOGY MAJOR; WHEREAS, I STUDIED ABROAD AND SHE TAUGHT ME EVERYTHING I KNOW! HOW WERE MY GRADES IN SCHOOL? EVERYTIME THEY GAVE US A BLOOD TEST, I ALWAYS GOT 'A PLUS; — CAN YOU SAY THAT?

- MY THESIS WAS IN WORLD GEOGRAPHY;
WHERE I CONVINCED ALL MY CLASSMATES AND TEACHERS;
THAT I HAD BEEN AROUND THE BLOCK A FEW TIMES
DURING THE TIME WHEN I WAS A MEMBER OF THE
WI-FI FRATERNITY. - PAPER TRIAL LEAD

TO MY GRADUATING FROM PROFESSIONAL BARTENDING SCHOOL; AND WORKED FOR THE MOST-PART OF THE NEXT 40 YEARS, INCOGNITO AS A SHRINK. - IN CHICAGO, L.A. RENO/SPARKS, THUS BECOMING MENTAL HEALTH CARES FINEST; OR BOOK PROOF THERE-OF IN HOW I BECAME ACCREDITED IN BECOMING YOUR NEW SIGMUND FREUD...

I'VE COME A LONG WAY FROM ONCE BEING CONSIDERED AS EMPLOYEE
OF THE MONTH AT DIAL-A-PRAYER. :)

FAKE NEWS (VS) YOURS TRULY.

THE REASON I DON'T HAVE OR OWN A GUN IS THAT THEY COST TO MUCH;
I'D PROBABLY HAVE TO GO OUT AND BUY ME A BRAND NEW TV, EVERYWEEK!!!

"All the News That's Fit to Print"

RIPE FOR JUDGEMENT "HOUSTON, I THINK WE HAVE A PROBLEM" 'EVERYONE WANTS TO FIND A NEW PLANET WHERE THEY CAN TAKE ALL THEIR SAME OLD SINS WITH THEM AND START LIFE OVER; WHEN IN FACT WE JUST NEED TO FIX THE ONE WE'RE ALREADY LIVING IN!

What ever happened to 'for the good of the country'?

SCHOOLED IN
G-E-E-K MYTHOLOGY
tells history from new view

THIS HERE BEING A NEW 'TRUE OR FALSE' NEWS PAPER TYPE QUIZ, OR
A ACCREDITED NEW COLLEGE COURSE ETC; FILLED WITH VOLUMES OF
WHO'S WHO, HISTORIC FIGURES.

SLANG WORD G-E-E-K,
'ORIGINALLY A DEROGATORY STAB'

DERIVED FROM ONE BEING A INTROVERTED, BOOKWORM STUDIOUS, INTELLECTUAL.

AUTHOR'S NOTE: YOURS TRULY, DEFINITION OF THE SLANG WORD G-E-E-K, IS -

A UNTREPRENEURIAL CREATIVE TYPE PERSON, IN A WORLD OF ONE'S OWN,
CONSIDERED TO BE SCHOLASTICALLY OR INNOVATIVELY IMAGINATIVE,
AND BENEFICIAL TO SOCIETY.

G-E-E-K MYTHOLOGY "EXAMPLE" TRUE OR FALSE? QUESTION!

DID FACE BOOK OWNER MARK ZUCKERBERG MARRY HIS ASIAN
WIFE,. BECAUSE HE WAS TIRED OF ORDERING STIR-FRY TAKE OUT???

— ANSWERS TO FALSE! 'THEREFORE,
THIS HERE BEING G-E-E-K MYTHOLOGY.

G-E-E-K MYTHOLOGY "EXAMPLE" TRUE OR FALSE? QUESTION!

"I AM 'NOT A CROOK" ☺
THE FORMER LATE, U.S. 37TH PRESIDENT RICHARD M. NIXON,
GOT HIS EARLY START IN POLITICS BY WAY OF WINNING $15,000
IN A CARD GAME; THEN USED THAT MONEY TOWARDS POLITICAL
ADVERTISMENT AND SIGNBOARD PROMOTION OF HIMSELF...
ANSWERS TO BEING TRUE!
THEREFORE THIS IS 'NOT G-E-E-K MYTHOLOGY.

TRUE OR FALSE? QUESTION!

APPEARANCE! - BEHIND HIS BACK, DID THE COMMON FOLK PEOPLE
ACCUSE OUR FIRST AMERICAN PRESIDENT GEORGE WASHINGTON, OF
BEING A CHAIN TOBACCO CHEWER? - BY WAY OF THEM HAVING NO
KNOWLEDGE ABOUT HIS WEARING OF 'WOODEN DENTURES?!...
"NO REPORTS OF ANY"
THEREFORE THIS IS FALSE! - OR G-E-E-K MYTHOLOGY.

BESIDES, BACK IN THOSE DAYS THEY USED 'SUPER POLLYANAN GRIP' FOR THEIR DENTURES.

TRUE OR FALSE? - AFTER BEING HOUNDED BY WOMEN; ROCK-STAR PAINTER, VINCENT
VANGOGH, CUT OFF HIS WEDDING RING FINGER TO SIGNAL TO WOMEN THAT HE WAS
NEVER GOING TO BE AVAILABLE FOR MARRIAGE? - ANSWERS TO FALSE, OR GEEK
MYTHOLOGY! - AS THE STORY ACTUALLY GOES HE WAS A MENTALLY UNSTABLE
RECLUSE, WHO CUT OFF HIS EAR...

A CURRICULUM PROPOSAL WITH ENDLESS SUBJECTS, AND
THE WIDENING OF ONE'S WHO'S WHO, KNOWLEDGE. THUS
BEING 'FUN IN EDUCATION...

WRITTEN BY: 'A EXTROVERTED GEEK...

EVERYONE'S TALKING ABOUT IT

FEATURING Telling the full story ●●● PAGE 21.

WHAT IF? WE DISCOVERED THAT HARVEY WEINSTEIN, WHEN
QUESTIONED, THOUGHT THAT ADULTERY WAS THE OLDEST TREE
GROWING IN HIS BACK-YARD! WHEREBY, WE NEED TO OPEN

THIS WHOLE CAN OF WORMS TO THE FULLEST EXTENT
IF WE'RE GOING TO BE CULTURALLY RECTIFYING
ALL OF CIVILIZATION.
IN BRIEF EXAMPLE: BETTER CLERGY?
DEVIL FORBID! WHAT IF?
'TO BECOME A CATHOLIC PRIEST ETC,
TO GET IN; YOU NOW HAVE TO SWEAR OFF CHILDREN,
AS OPPOSED TO WOMEN!
-SO MUCH FOR THE 'QUIT YOUR GRIN'IN AND DROP YOUR LINEN
OL' CLICHE. -ALONG WITH A STIFF PENCIL HAS 'NO CONSCIOUS,
YOUR HONOR! 'IS NOW 'OFFICIALLY INEXCUSABLE...

'TIME AND PLACE FOR EVERY WARDROBE'

LET'S GO FROM THE # ME TOO GAME;
TO THE # TAUNTING GAME!

"STILL NO EXCUSE FOR SEXUAL MISCONDUCT".
CLUELESS TAUNTING BY WOMEN, IS WHEN THEY
ARE INAPPROPRIATELY DRESSED TO SEXY
FOR THE OCCASION;
THAT CAN LEAD TO THIS AN EFFECT.
IN HINDSIGHT A HOW TO:
MAKE GUY'S ACKNOWLEDGE YOU FOR YOUR
'NANCY PELOSI WARDROBE; SHOULD YOU
WANT TO BE LOOKED UPON AND ACKNOWLEDGED
FOR WHAT'S BETWEEN YOUR EARS, AS OPPOSED TO
WHAT'S BETWEEN YOUR ARM PITS.'ETC'
'EVERYBODY IS SELLING SOMETHING' AS FOR
ME, I'M JUST PROMOTING MY NEW-AGE BIBLE MOVEMENT!
'WAR PAINT AT DAWN OVER KILL? 'YOUR CALL!!!
IN CONCLUSION: EVERYONE HAS A POTENTIAL 'GOOD BOOK IN THEM;
IF THEY COULD ONLY FIND A GOOD INTERPRETER●

AUTHOR'S NOTE: THE ONLY TIME I'VE EVER BEEN ACCUSED OF ANY
KIND OF SEXUAL HARRASMENT; IS WHEN I WAS PLAYING IN A GAME
OF CHARADES AND WAS GIVEN THE WORD 'LAKE TITICACA' TO TRY
AND PANTOMIME!!! ☺

'Time f∘r small thinking is ∘ver,'

'Life according to a new modern DAY CLEAN SLATE.'

11/17 **IN THE NEWS** 11/17

(((SEXUAL MISCONDUCT EPIDEMIC))) PAGE 22.

TODAY'S MOST-WANTED ARTICLES. FACTS ON FILE **Make an Impact**

"TODAY'S NEW-AGE 'LIVING BIBLE"
(VERSUS)
YESTERDAY'S OLD SCHOOL:

- AS WE LEARN ABOUT IN 'IMPACTIVE MONKEY WRENCH THROWING 101':
ABOUT ONE'S MORAL I.Q. TEST EVALUTION. E-X-A-M-P-L-E

☑ CHECK THE APPROPRIATE BOX IN DECLARING
'YOUR ASSESSMENT OF WHICH IS
'THE GREATER OF SIN'?
= MAKE THIS YOUR MOMENT.

EATING SINFULLY DELICIOUS B.B.Q RIBS! ☐ ((OR))

PHYSICALLY GROPING AN UN-ACCOMMODATING FEMALE! ☑

EATING A 'BLT' SANDWICH! ☐ ((OR))

PHYSICALLY GROPING AN UN-ACCOMMODATING MALE! ☑

EATING BREAKFAST PORK SAUSAGE! ☐ ((OR))

SEXUALLY HARASSING SOMEONE WHO HAS 'NO INTENTION OF

'EVER GOING SKINNY DIPPING WITH YOU. ☑

'VANITY' - COSMETIC SURGERY, AND THE WHOLE 9 YARDS! ☐ ((OR))

ALL THE ASPECTS OF 'BULLING'! ☑

'SAVING FACE' **REMEDIE** 'LET THERE BE A VIABLE
"O-P-T-I-O-N"!!!

'LEGALIZE 'WIND UP DOLL ON CALL, OR IN HOUSE PROSTITUTION!!!
LET THERE BE LIKE ONLY ONE TYPE OF SEX HAPPENING ON THE PLANET;
C-O-N-S-E-N-S-U-A-L AND TO DO THAT WE NEED TO
"LEGALIZE PROSTITUTION"
"IN RETROSPECT NO MORE EXCUSES"...

IN CONCLUSION: THERE'S 90, MILES OF DIFFERENCE IN BIG BUCKS HUSH MONEY
PAID TO ACCUSERS; THAN SLAM, BANG, THANK YOU MAM, PROSTITUTION; ((OR))
HOW ONE —— STAYS RICH AND TIGHT WAD ☺ ...

Miss ONE page and you miss a lot

TAKING STOCK OF statement Resolutions put on paper; pastor thinking outside the box!

* IN BRIEF:

TO ALL THE PEOPLE OUT THERE THAT ARE OPPOSED TO
THE 'LEGALIZATION OF PROSTITUTION'! GEAR UP FOR 'YOUR'
NOW NEW-AGE MORALITY SOCIETY! - NO MORE SUGAR DADDIES,
TROPHY WIVES, THUS NO MORE MARRYING SOMEONE BY WAY OF
THE 'WORLD'S OLDEST PROFESSION' "FOR THEIR MONEY".
'EVERYTHING IN LIFE IS TO A DEGREE' WHEREAS,
'BIG BROTHER SUBJECTS' YOU'LL NOW BE ASSIGN
TO A MARRIAGE BALANCED ECONOMIC ASSESSMENT CONCILIAR,
FOR YOUR MARRIAGE LEGITIMACY. ☺
'SO TO SPEAK, NEW-AGE MORALITY SOCIETY?!
- MANY A 'SAME 'STORY EXAMPLE OUT THERE
TO HAVING A 'NO THERAPEUTIC ACCESS
FOR A -CHO-SEUNG-HUI-KILL-32-;
WHO WAS A SEX DRIVEN CRAZED 'VIRGIN,
IN PERSUIT OF BECOMING A
'I'LL JUST PAY FOR IT' ROLL IN THE HAY
* REJECT ●
'THUS RESULTING IN HIM BECOMING A KILLING MACHINE.
FURTHERMORE, WITH THE 'HISTORY OF ALL THE SEXUALLY
ASSAULTED VULNERABLE WOMEN IN THE U.S. MILITARY;
JUST THE SAME, TOSS IN ALL THE COLLEGE CAMPUS
'LOWER EDUCATION''GO FOR IT' ACCESSIBILE COVER-UP FACILITIES.
WHEREBY, IN TAKING AWAY ALL THE DIM-WIT PREDATORS EXCUSES;
THERE'S NO EXCUSE FOR THAT KIND OF MISCREANT BEHAVIOR
ANYMORE...
'SUMMERY, SUMMARY' IN CONCLUSION:
"LEGALIZE PROSTITUTION"

Based on Notebooks 'Plan for Prosperity'

As Book lovers gear up for sale —— PAGE 23.

Book store: How a Blockbuster Was Born ●●●

'MONK AMONG YOU'

lifestyle OnAssignment

OR " RELIGIOUSLY MARRIED to my VOCATION."

process clarify / obligation with God., meets

with clients. meets with unlimited.'A EVERY

DAY intimate LOVING RELATIONSHIP is

a matter of Having adequate time!

(First draft of An event is born)

true PREPARATION Can find a place for Love

and Romance In This a BUSY LIFESTYLE!

Who's Tha Right One For You ?

Help Wanted: needed A Unique COVER GIRL

Attraction with 'Adaptation' of turning into

A Multitasker LIVE-IN SECRETARY-MAID

and then some., `Can you hear me now

Girl Friend'. WHAT NO TAKERS ? PAGE BUNNY RANCH.

RENO NEVADA, He's not worried-Go for

plan B, backup project Proposal!

DOCTOR'S BOOK OF NEW World REMEDIES

IT'S A NO-BRAINER ... PAGE 24.

" When words need to be said "
The Future of earth balance democracy is at stake.

Report places blame for Climate change global warming squarely on humans

Greenhouse gas emissions likely 'dominant cause'

(((QUESTIONING AUTHORITY)))

'SO YESTERDAY' FOR THEIR FAILURE TO RECOGNIZE THE 'EQUAL IMPACT OF –

What EVERYONE ON EARTH Needs to KNOW.

Birth control is A Realistic Survival Plan.

"OVERPOPULATION IS A MAJOR IN-GREEDY-ENT TO GLOBAL WARMING CLIMATE CHANGE"

SCIENCE, **lack of ability to go deep leading to**

hellish conditions

Libra (Sept. 23-Oct. 23).
The advances in thought come when you mix categories.

: Earth in danger earth at stake.

'WITH EXAMPLE OF WARM WATER HURRICANES, DEATH ☹ AND DISTRUCTION $$$

time to calculate the costs?

Point-of-View *'PRO-LIFE GOES INTO EFFECT THE DAY PRO-INTELLIGENCE, (BIRTH CONTROL) COMES OF AGE.*

'CHOOSE *PRO-INTELLIGENCE.'*

OF Paradise & Poverty

IRRESPONSIBILITY CULMINATES TO THIS HERE BEING A GLOBAL RESOURCE EXHAUSTING 'BABY FACTORY' POVERTY STRICKEN OVER-LOAD OF =BIBLICAL PROPORTIONS=! -FETUS-FEED-US-FEET-US- (SHOES, etc. -FEAT-US-(JOBS, JOBS, JOBS,).

2012, THERE'S NO SUCH THING AS OVER-POPULATION AND PIECE ON EARTH; THE MORE THE SCARIER. (EXAMPLE) 'ARAB SPRING' IN SYRIA, 'ETC! IN REFERENCE TO THE KILLING OF ALL THOSE PEOPLE'-IN NOT BEING ABLE TO PROVIDE FOR THEIR WANTS AND NEEDS, THEY ALL BECAME 'EQIVALENT' TO A HOUSE CLEANING LATE TERM ABORTION; ALONG WITH ALL THE MULTITUDES OF TENT CITY REFUGEES, THAT ARE ALL PRODUCTS OF 'OVERPOPULATION' THUS AN UN-ACHIEVABLE QUALITY OF LIFE'S WORST NIGHTMARE!

SETTING THE BAR. IN RETROSPECT OF HOW 'NOT TO BECOME A CONTRIBUTING FACTOR TO THE OVERPOPULATION, DIRT POOR POVERTY SOCIETY!? 'MASTURBATION IS THE GRANDIS FORM OF BIRTH CONTROL' AND IN THIS HERE RELIGION, IT'S ONLY A SIN IF YOU GET CAUGHT...

Poor People's Campaign
To the letter

NEW-AGE PHILOSOPHY PROPHECY,'SHOULD THIS BE YOU'
FEATURING THE BABY FACTORY, TOTAL IRRESPONSIBILTY
S-I-N-DROME PLAYERS!
DOES THIS NEEDLE POINT TO YOU?
'THUS BEING A MISERY LOVES COMPANY CONTRIBUTOR.
WHEREAS, BRINGING SOMEONE AS LIKE IN YOURSELF,
INTO THIS WORLD THAT WILL ALWAYS HAVE TO STRUGGLE
FOR FOOD, CLOTHING, SHELTER, ETC, VIA
THE WHOLE QUALITY OF LIFE PACKAGE.

Call Time Out!

'BIRTH CONTROL IS A
REALISTIC DIFFERENCE MAKER'

- OR -

WELCOME TO 'HELL'
MAKE SURE THEY ISSUE YOU
A PITCH'FORK...

THEREFORE, GO FORTH AND MULTIPY THIS PHILOSOPHY
AND THE VALUE OF 'YOUR LIFE AND PROSPERITY
WILL EVENTUALLY BECOME UP-GRADED
- TO THE HURRAY FOR ME,'I GOT MINE
SOCIETY; AS OPPOSED TO THE 'HELLISH
- 'YOU GET TO SUFFER, SUFFER , TILL YOU DIE SOCIETY.
'WHY BE STUCK IN THIS VIRTUAL MINIMUM WAGE,
WAREHOUSE POOL OF = OVERPOPULATION, GREENHOUSE GASSES,
RESOURCE EXHAUSTING 'THE BEAT GOES ON' OVERLOAD ;
WHERE THE EMPLOYER, HAS THE VAST LUXURY OF PICK AND
CHOOSE PERSONEL; WHEN 'YOU CAN HAVE THE LESS SUPPLY
THE MORE DEMAND LUXURY OF EVENTUALLY ENTERING INTO
THE 'HURRAY FOR ME,'I GOT MINE SOCIETY' THAT FORMULATES
$EQUALITY... AUTHOR'S NOTE: "GLOBALLY SPEAKING"
'QUALITY OF LIFE 'IN YOUR DREAMERS?
THIS HERE ESSAY WAS WRITTEN 'BECAUSE OF THIS HERE
ISSUE OF TOO MUCH PLANETARY
= YOU SUFFER, YOU SUFFER, TILL YOU DIE ...
'FOR THOSE OF YOU THAT LOVE KIDS SO MUCH; 'THERE'S A SPECIAL
PLACE IN HEAVEN' THAT GOD, PUT YOU ON THIS EARTH TO PERFORM;
IT'S CALLED SCHOOL TEACHER...PAGE 26.

FRIAR FLYER 'FEATURING STATIONS OF THE DOUBLE CROSSED'... PAGE 27.

FAITH FORUM **RENO GAZETTE-JOURNAL** APRIL/2017 YOURS TRULY, RESPONSE TO

What's the coolest story from scripture?

JESUS, AT 'THE LAST SUPPER' AFTER DRINKING HIS FILL OF MAD DOG 20/20 WINE, OR ENOUGH TO GET A OVER TWICE THE ALCOHOL LIMIT DONKEY DRIVING D.U.I. STATES TO HIS APOSTLES. (JESUS) MIRACLES!!?? IF WALKING ON -ICE- OR A WATER WASN'T GOOD ENOUGH FOR THE ROMANS TO MAKE THEM A BELIEVER OF ME; "WAIT TILL I SHOW THEM HOW I CAN WALK ALL OVER BUREAUCRATIC GRID'LOCK; THAT'S THE MIRACLE I'M TALKING ABOUT!" THE LEAST POLITICAL WORD EVER USED IN WASHINGTON IS CALLED BIPARTISANSHIP; AND I PLAN ON CHANGING THAT BY INVENTING TOP 'ROMAN NOODLES!'IN TWO YEARS I'LL BE OLD ENOUGH TO RUN FOR PRESIDENT AND I'M GOING TO PICK THAT ASS-WHOLE ✱ KANYE, TO BE MY VICE-PRESIDENT; JUST TO PROVE THAT EVERYONE WILL STILL VOTE FOR ME...

   - PRIOR TO BEING APPREHENDED BY THE AUTHORTIES, AS THE STORY GOES-THAT'S WHEN JESUS PLOTED TO OVER'THROW THE ROMAN GOVERNMENT IN NEED OF HELP-ING THE POOR, BY WAY OF TELLING PONTIUS PILOT, THAT 'HE WAS GOD IN THE FLESH' - AND PILOT'S RESPONSE TO HIM WAS - YOU GUYS ARE A DIME A DOZEN; 'YOU, JIM JONES, DAVID KORESH, CHARLES MAN-SON! - AND JESUS RESPONDS - BUT WAIT A MIN-UTE , I'M THE MESSIAH; AND PILOT SAID PROVE IT?! 'JESUS THEN RESPONDS 'HE WHO IS WITHOUT SIN, CAST THE FIRST NECULAR WARHEAD!!! - FEELING INTIMATED, AND IGNORANT TO THE SITUATIONAL UP-GRADE, PILOT SAYS - CRUCIFY HIM - ...

- JUST DOWN THE STREET WHERE JUDAS WHO DIDN'T BUY INTO THE STORY; THUS RE-CEIVED MONEY FOR RATTING ON JESUS; THEN OUT OF HIS GUILT TOOK THAT MONEY AND BET IT ALL ON THE GONZAGA JESUITS, IN HONOR OF JESUS, TO WIN THE 2017, COLL-EGE BASKETBALL NATIONAL CHAMPIONSHIP GAME - AND FINAL SCORE, HANGED HIMSELF.
- IN THIS HERE DEVELOPING STORY; MARY MAGDALENE, IN SEARCH OF FINDING JESUS, FINALLY FINDS HIM AT THE CROSS. MARY SPEAKING, 'THE PEOPLE WERE ALL TELLING ME THAT THEY SAW YOU, AND THAT YOU GOT HAMMERED; I THOUGHT THAT THEY WERE ALL TALKING ABOUT AT THE 'LAST SUPPER' WHERE YOU TURNED WINE INTO WATER! - SO WHAT DID YOU DO TO DESERVE ALL THIS? - AND JESUS RESPONDS, HONEY 'I SHRUNK' THE KIDS! - "ALL GOD'S CHILDREN"... - MEAN WHILE, ON THE OTHER SIDE OF TOWN WHERE APOSTLE PETER, THE FIRST POPE 'WHO WAS A <u>FISHERMAN</u> WITH NO SHORTAGES OF TELLING <u>WHOPPERS</u> WAS SELLING HIS STORY OF ADVANTAGES TO THE ONE % ERS! 'PETER SPEAKING, THIS WAY THERE'S ONLY 'ONE UNIQUE 'SON OF GOD' HERO HERE, THAT'S JESUS! - AND 'ALL YOU GUYS GET TO HERD YOUR WEALTH WITHOUT ANY GUILT. OR BACK'LASH; THUS LEAVING THE REST OF SOCIETY OUT THERE IN BEING CONSIDERED AS NOTHING MORE THAN A BUNCH OF <u>BARGAINLESS</u>

'Nobodies.'

I'LL EVEN TOSS IN 'HE DIED FOR YOUR SIN' IT'S IMPRESSIVE TO ALL THE SIMPLE MINDED PEOPLE OUT THERE! - ONE % ERS RESPONDING, AND WE'LL MAKE SURE THAT YOUR ORGANIZATION 'NEVER HAS TO PAY ANY TAXES! ☺ DEAL ...

IN CONCLUSION: THE GENESIS OF REAL NEWS (VS) FAKE —YOU BE THE JUDGE;

'closing into the gap between rich & poor; thus creation of a conscious'!!!

AUTHOR'S NOTE: - AS A YOUTH GROWING UP I, WAS SENTENCED TO DOING A 8, YEAR STINT IN A PAROCHICAL SCHOOL; I PAID MY DEBT TO SOCIETY; WHEREAS THIS IS WHERE ALL THIS THOUGHT PROVOKING INFORMATION DERIVED FROM...

✱ NAME CALLING, WORTHY FROM THE TAYLOR SWIFT PARALLAX ORDEAL, THAT TOOK PLACE ETC.

THE REASON YOU NEVER HEARD THAT MUCH IN THE BIBLE
ABOUT JOSEPH THE FATHER OF JESUS, IS THAT WHEN HE AND MOTHER
MARY WENT TO DIVORCE COURT; HE TOLD THE JUDGE THAT 'JESUS WAS BORN
OF A VIRGIN' SO THAT HE COULD GET OUT OF PAYING ANY KIND OF CHILD
SUPPORT; HE ACTUALLY WAS THE FIRST ONE WHO COIN PHRASED THE STATEMENT
'I DID NOT HAVE SEX WITH THAT WOMAN' AND THE REST IS BIBLICAL HISTORY.. ☺

experience a renaissance
Rewriting Life Stories
aims to 'revitalize' society

THE 'HIGH PRIORITIES' OF THIS MAN'S RELIGION, FOCUSES ON THOU SHELT NOT - 'INSTIGATE - KILL' FACTOR., ALONG WITH (INITIAL) PAGE **ON** GREED. 'WHEREAS THIS IS HOW ONE BEHAVIORALLY LEGITIMATIZES, IN HAVING A REALISTIC PRAYER RAPOR **WITH** God.' Amen.

- ARE YOU AWARE THAT IN THE 'BIG' PICTURE OF LIFE, ONLY A TRUE "PREDOMINANTLY POSITIVE SPIRIT FILLED, GOD LOVING, PROGRAMED PERSON" 'WOULD ONLY KILL IN SELF-DEFENSE, WAR OR JUSTIFIABLE CAPITAL PUNISHMENT $.

""PRODUCTS OF OUR ENVIRONMENT""
HUMAN BEANS, PLANTED SEEDS, POTENTIAL ANYTHINGS,
'WITHOUT POSITIVE DOMINANT FEEDBACK...

'WAKE UP AND SMELL THE C-O-P-Y'

MINUS - THE SEX-OFFENDERS, DRUG PUSHERS,
BULLIES, RACIST, AND CON-ARTIST, ETC.
'IT TAKES WHAT'S LEFT OF A VILLAGE'.

Reality Check BIG GOTCHA!!!

WITH ALL THOSE 'NEAR DEATH EXPERIENCE' CONFESSORS OUT THERE; REMINISCING ON HOW THEY VIRTUALLY SAT ON JESUS' LAP AND ATE PANCAKES --- AFTER ALL THESE YEARS WHY HASN'T THERE EVER BEEN ANYONE OUT THERE PROCLAIMING THAT THEY WERE PAINFULLY' DANCING WITH THA DEVIL ON RED HOT COALS IN PITHFORK CITY??? DON'T LOOK AT ME!

"Based on logic."

"BIRTH IS TERMINAL - AND YOU ONLY GO AROUND ONCE! WE'RE ALL VISITORS OF THIS PLANET, PLAN IT! WRITTEN BY YOURS TRULY, 1980. "WE ALL LIVE TO BE SOMEBODYS MEMORIES! - AND "WE'RE ALL SNOWMEN UNDER SUN LAMPS!

= CAN I GET A WITNESS =

whereas people come in all kinds of colors,
shapes and sizes; be nice to them all! One 'mind' fits all...

FOR THE RECORD Once Upon A Time,
Who Knew What, and When?
"Pardons DESIGN To Rule." PAGE 28.

WAR AND REMEMBRANCE *Great Getaways*

'PARALLEL PHENOMENOM DISCOVERY KIT' - AS WE TAKE A STERN LOOK
AT THIS NEW KID ON THE BLOCK' YOURS TRULY, THE LINK THAT'S
GOING TO LINE YOU, IS NOW THE LINE THAT'S GOING TO LINK YOU.
THE COACH OF THE HORSES, OR THE WORK'HORSE THAT ISN'T A PHONY.
ELOQUENTLY BEING THE STAGE WITHIN YOUR WORLD THAT HAS A GOOD
PART FOR EVERYBODY. (COMMON PARALLEL) BY THIS HERE BOOK AUTHOR:
'GREEN HAM & SIDEWALK EGGS' - A HARD BOILED LOOK AT 'POVERTY
FROM A, 'MAN DOESN'T LIVE BY' FOOD STAMPS ALONE, PERSPECTIVE!
(FOLKLORE DISAGREEMENT EXAMPLE) "HE DIED FOR OUR SINS" SPOOF
- AS LIKE IN THIS PORTRAYAL - A SERIAL BANK ROBBER DEFENDANT
IN COURT; FACES A DEVOTE CHRISTIAN JUDGE, AND MAKES THIS
COMMENT TO HIM! - YOUR HONOR, "HE DIED FOR OUR SINS" - AND
PROCEEDS TO WALK RIGHT OUT OF THE COURT ROOM A FREE MAN. ☺
FURTHERMORE, ANYONE THAT'S EVER DIED IN A WAR FOR THE
'LACK OF SKILLFUL DIPLOMACY; "DIED FOR OUR SINS" 'ETC'.
- ALL WITHIN A NEW-AGE BIBLICAL ACCORDANCE TO = A
LARRY CHRISTMAS TO YOU!!!
- WHEREAS, I WAS BORN OF A VIRGIN;
FOR MY MOTHER WAS ONCE A VIRGIN'.
'THUS HOW A STORK BOUND CHRISTMAS DAY DELIVERY,
BECOMES A PULLING SOME FEATHERS
'STOP THE WORLD I WANT TO GET ON'
7 MONTH, PREMO-BABY; 'COMPATABLE TO ALL'
LIBRA SCALE BRAIN, LEFTY!
'TRUTH IS STRANGER THAN FICTION'
IN PAVING THE WAY FOR MY COMING INTO THIS WORLD!
(RIGHT OF PASSAGE, DISTINCTION.)
(WW2, ENGLAND.)
WHERE MY STATIONED IN ENGLAND FATHER, A U.S.
AIR FORCE OFFICER, AND A GENTLEMAN'; MET MY BRITISH
MOTHER AT A DANCE; STARTED DATING AND GOT MARRIED.
'SO THEN ON HONEYMOON NIGHT THEY GOT A HOTEL ROOM ON
THE OTHER SIDE OF TOWN, AND WERE ABOUT TO SETTLE IN
FOR THE EVENING WHEN MY MOTHER STATED TO MY FATHER.
I, FORGOT ONE OF MY SUITCASES. 'SO MY GRACIOUS
FATHER, A SOLID CITIZEN GAVE IT THE OL'
'WE AIN'T LEFT YET! - SO WHEN THEY RETURNED TO THEIR
HOTEL THAT SAME EVENING; ONLY TO FIND OUT THAT IT WAS
'HITLER AIR BOMB BLOWN TO SMITHEREENS,
AND EVERYBODY IN THE BUILDING WAS KILLED...
IN CONCLUSION: THIS IS WHERE THE LEGENDARY ROOTS OF THIS
RELIGION ACTUALLY STARTED! VALIDATES THIS HERE
'TIS THE SEASON, LARRY CHRISTMAS TO YOU'... PAGE 29.

VALIDATION TIME FOR
'REVOLUTIONARY PREACHER'

Intelligent design CONTINUED =

'BY WAY OF GOD PULLING THE MATCH-MAKING MATRIMONIAL STRINGS;
THUS REASON - YOURS TRULY - BECAME A MULTICULTURAL - HISPANIC
- ARAB - JEW - WITH THAT IN MIND COULD GIVE ME, THE 'POTENTIAL
OF CONVERTING 'ALL OF CHRISTIANITY, AND ISLAM, "ETC" OR SIX
BILLION PEOPLE "PLUS" 'THAT COULD' CULTURALLY CLAIM 'ME AS
BEING ONE OF THEIR'S; AND THE REST OF HUMANITY JUST BEING IN
IT FOR THE 'HIGHWAY TO HEAVEN ON EARTH' AMBIENCE. - REPENT ☺

"THIS HERE BEING A 'PEACE ON EARTH,'ONE WORLD RELIGION'

'RIGHTEOUSLY COMBATING MADNESS'

'ARGABALLY SPEAKING, WE 'ALL NEED TO BE ON
THE "SAME PAGE" OF RUDIMENTARY SANITY'...

♫ TO MANY CHURCHS, AND NOT ENOUGH TRUTH! ♫

bull-riding winner

"I WAS RAISED TO RESPECT MY ELDERS 'BUT
WHEN IT COMES TO BEING CONFRONTED WITH NEANDERTHALISM?!
- WRITTEN BY MAN, INSPIRED BY GOD:

IS 'NOW HOT OFF THE PRESS"...

BIG-TIME INSPIRATION

"This is what 'I was put on earth to do".

Lessons learned from <u>Positive</u> INFLUENCE

"SOMEONE" ONCE SAID THAT LIFE IS UNFAIR; 'THEREFORE
I'M JUST HERE TO EVEN THE SCORE"...

ONE CENT
WE NEED YOU!

(YOURS TRULY, IS AN AMERICAN BORN; U.S. ARMY DRAFTED VETERAN. PAGE 30.

'STARTING OVER! - COMING OUT OF THE DARK AGES - ANYONE?

THE BIBLE & QURAN ACCORDING TO A CONCLUSION!

PUBLISHERS CLEARING HOUSE 'TWO FOR ONE CLOSEOUT SALE.

Say It Ain't So, Reality Check **Tha Party's Over.**

NOTE:'THA=MAN,'THE=GOD.

Time to Rescue *tha* NEANDERTHAL DISCRIMINATORY *Once Upon A Time Bible'* ETC,ETC.

- FOR 'ALL' INSPIRATIONAL AND INGENIOUS PROPHETS; <u>WILL BE UPDATED AND ETERNALLY OPEN</u>. 'FORMULA TO PROPHECY DECLARED DEAD AWAKEN TO A NEW LIFE.

(WRITTEN IN 1983, BY YOURS TRULY THA COMMISSIONER.)

'ANNOUNCING AUTHENTIC BIBLE PROPHECY, "YOU CAN BUY IN" HISTORY MADE AVAILABLE TO YOU. MAGIC KINGDOM CLUB SPOTLIGHT ON EXTRA BUNDLES! PASSING OF TIME 'SINS' WILL SOON BE FORGIVEN...

'Life according to IF 'I CAN ((<u>TURN</u>)) A BUS LOAD OF TOP DOG 1% er's ((<u>STONE</u>)) FACES ((<u>INTO</u>)) A SMILE, THENCE BE PLENTY ENOUGH ((<u>BREAD</u>)) TO GO AROUND FOR EVERYBODY!!!

WORLD'S FIRST TRILLIONAIRE??? SIGNED: THA OBLIGATORY 'ROBIN HOOD; ASTUTE IN HANDING OUT 'QUALITY OF LIFE' PACKAGING; ETC "THAT FOR 'HIS TRUE LOVE OF GOD' WILL DAMN NEAR DIE BROKE". - NOW GET OUT THERE AND PASS 'THAT COLLECTION PLATE AROUND. ··

Bible **Deciphering** reform plan

1989. <u>quote John Shelby Spong</u>. Episcopal bishop of Newark, New Jersey.

RE-EDITED MUCH "improved" *version of Written* BY *YOURS TRULY.*

THA LITTERAL INTERPETATIOINS OF THA BIBLE HAVE FOSTERED SOME OF THA MOST HIDEOUS OF INSTITUTIONS SUCH AS WAR AND REVENGE. 'MANY A CASE OF SOLE SEARCHING DELUSIONAL PSYCOTIC CRIME, SUCH AS JIM JONES, OR DAVID KORESH, ETC.' INFERIOR FUROR, OR THA HITLER BIBLE READING COURSE OF 'CHOSEN PEOPLE' ANTI-SEMITISM. THA SUBJUGATION OF WOMEN. HOMOPHOBIA. CONDONATION OF SLAVERY VIA ECONOMIC OPPRESSION. 'A BOOK RESPONSIBLE FOR THESE STATEMENTS THUS INACTMENTS, CANNOT BE IN ANY LITERAL SENSE THE TRUE WORD OF **God.**

"IN THAT THA BIBLE IS ALL IN ALL MORE ANCIENT HUMAN STANDARD CREATED THEN GOD INSPIRED. CONSPICUOUSLY THA BIBLE IS A BOOK OF SYMBOLIC RATHER THEN LITERAL VERSES, OR UNSCIENTIFIC ILLOGICAL HUMAN FABLES TOLD THRU OLD-TIME MORAL PRECEPTS. THEREFORE IN NEED OF LIBERATION FROM ITS OWN TEACHINGS, TO BE UPDATED AND REWRITTEN FOR THA PEOPLE OF OUR TIMES, AND ALL TIMES'... PAGE 31.

Ancient Sunni Shiite divide
discussion in moral terms
~Quran/

RIGHT WHERE THEY LEFT OFF
Doctor's Shocking Revelation

" FEATURING SECTARIAN RACISM "

A lot of people won't even realize the truth of the situation until you point it out.

(((LABELED AS RACISM)))

MOSQUE MADNESS, 'REPAIR KIT' '72 VERSIONS OF "ONLY TRUTH CAN FREE YOU"!

'STRATEGY' THAT SHOULD BE HIGHLY CONSIDERED!!!

The art of restoring magnetic heads — People,

to be a card carrying member of the 'true family of ALLAH ;

there are no ethnical RACE, CREED, OR COLOR. **differences** •

" WHEREAS TO FIND 'POSITIVE SAMENESS' WITHIN YOUR FELLOW MAN 'IS TO FIND HEAVEN ON EARTH' S-A-N-E-N-E-S-S = AMEN "

Introducing **The world according to** THE 'MAHDI'

♩ COME TOGETHER RIGHT NOW, OVER ME...

The book on 'Remove all doubt'
NO LOOKING BACK. PAGE 32.

WORLD'S #1 CONDITIONER

"BOOK'S PARALLEL EPILOGUE: AND DEAR GOD, NO NEED TO FORGIVE ANYONE NOW = FOR THEY KNOW NOW WHAT THEY DO!".

FAITH FORUM QUESTION ON:

MOST INSPIRING RELIGIOUS FIGURE? ANSWERS TO

" ALL THIS HASN'T BEEN GIVEN TO ME FOR NOTHING."

♫ THE FINAL COUNT DOWN ♫

BORN ON A BIO ♫ *"It's The End Of World As We Know It"*

The world according to DR. SUNDAY,

'MAKE A DIFFERENCE ENDER'S GAME'

'<u>POLICE</u> STATE' THAT THE DOCTOR WILL SEE YOU NOW...

'political religious revolution'

Guidelines: "PEACEFUL 'EVOLUTION, REVOLUTION, IS THE SOLUTION TO BE FREE OF MENTAL POLUTION."

"PATRIOTISM IS THE BACKBONE OF OUR COUNTRY! YOURS TRULY, BEST RESTORER OF."

THE SEARCH FOR SIGNS OF INTELLIGENT LIFE IN THE UNIVERSE

YOUR GUIDE TO *The Real Day The Earth Stood Still* ((COUNTDOWN))

OUTTA THIS WORLD AND ON WITH THE NEXT..

'WILL OF GOD TESTIMONY' TAKES 'YOU TO ME LEADER!

'ALIEN LINGUAL ▄ 'DIT JUNEAU RAT NOW, DAT OLIVE IN WE KNOW!

♫ MEET THE NEW BOSS - 'NOT' THE SAME AS THE OLD BOSS..

rhetoric of revolution **I specialize in solutions!**

"FOR WHAT STARTED WITH 'RELIGION, CAN ONLY BE 'RECTIFIED BY RELIGION!!!"

You are now officially out of excuses, "THY WILL BE DONE."

BETTER LIVING THROUGH DISCOVERY

FINALLY... <u>LIFE</u> INSURANCE YOU CAN AFFORD

'WAKE UP AND SMELL THE C-O-P-Y' OF A Democracy Prison Original.

IN BRIEF: HOW TO SAY SOMETHING IN SO MANY WORDS.

<u>EXPERIENCE HAVING A BEAUTIFUL MIND.</u>

- IN TEACHING PEOPLE HOW TO BECOME 'FRA<u>N</u>K WITHOUT THE BUN!

DR. SUNDAY *Discovery Kit* PAGE 33.

((ANSWERS TO MYSTERIOUS END OF AN AGE PROPHECY FULFILLED))

OR ` HELL, WHAT'S A NICE GUY LIKE ME DOING IN A PLACE LIKE THIS?

Representatives represent
WANTED
New leader, new nation, new world!
A UNIQUE SOURCE OF SUPERIOR WISDOM.
Someone must stand up to our government.
WE'RE NOT GONNA TAKE IT Anymore
BEGINS HERE! PAGE 34.

♫ Give'em some of that <u>new</u>-time religion
...And They Lived Happily Ever After."

WHO AM I??? I'M YOUR 'WALK IN MY SHOES' P-L-E-A-S-E, 'MESSIAH!

IN BRIEF: WHO AM I??? I'M THE GLOBAL WOMENS RIGHTS ABRAHAM LINCOLN.
WHO AM I? I'M YOUR MINIMUM WAGE LAW IS NOTHING MORE THAN A
FANCY NAME FOR SLAVERY = CLAIMS ADJUSTER...
WHO AM I? I'M YOUR WINNING LOTTERY TICKET OUT OF HELL'GUIDE.
WHO AM I? 'I REALIZE PEOPLE DON'T KNOW ME FROM ADAM;
AND YET I AM THE NEW WORLD ADAM!!!

`WORLD IN CRISIS` WHO AM I??? THE CATASTROPHIC DIFFERENCE MAKER SPOKESPERSON OF
"HE WHO IS WITHOUT SIN CAST THE FIRST NUCLEAR WARHEAD"·

<u>The real deal</u>, is now Stand and deliver
Don't deprive me of my right to be `YOU CAN'T FAKE`

F-O-R REPLACEMENT C-H-R-I-S-T S-A-K-E, YOURS TRULY "THE
CHOSEN ONE MESSIAH CLASSROOM SAVIOR OF THE WORLD!"

OUTTA THIS WORLD AND ON WITH THE NEXT **READY OR NOT, DAY HAS ARRIVED.**

The world is waiting, Inquiring Minds Want to Know:
"ALL GOD'S CHILDREN, HISTORIC INAUGURAL DECLARATION".

♫ # WON'T GET FOOLED AGAIN.

First Amendment
Rights ⟶
WATCHA WAITIN' FOR.

TOO LEGIT TO QUIT
Project Restart! # HIS TIME IS now.

'THIS THING IS NOT OVER'
When words need to be said
The
CHRONICLES
of
Dr. Sunday

TIME CAPSULE Reality Check

10/20/46

What's News ! Bible revision **Caveman** Extremists **Smoke and Mirrors Roll Over** Convention , CLEARANCE SALE.

Come out of the Dark Ages.

"Presenting GOD'S INSPIRED WORD." PAGE 35.

Writer traces roots of religion

"FOR WHAT STARTED WITH 'RELIGION, CAN ONLY BE 'RECTIFIED BY RELIGION!!!"

"IN BRIEF: *Life according to* **a new modern**

DAY <u>RELIGIOUS</u> CLEAN SLATE."

exemplifies What you needed to know **AND** Process.

Life Lessons as Timeless as Infinity

"Storytelling on a grand scale"

THE POSITIVE Faith Religion

Laying Claim to Ministry of Higher Education ...

A UNIQUE SOURCE **of** SUPERIOR WISDOM

Religious Science training program

New Age **Make a difference** Bible School

THE <u>ONE</u> and only GOD

PERFORMS <u>MIRACLES</u>. 'NOT' STRUCTTLED MAN.,
BUT THROUGH MAN BY <u>GOD</u>. NOW THAT'S
THE **POSITIVE** <u>SPIRIT.</u>

--EXAMPLE

THA MIRACLE OF MODERN DAY MEDICINE, AVIATION, 'UNDER-
STANDING' -ETC-ETC-ETC-ETC-ETC- GOD <u>WORKING THRU MAN.</u>

DR. SUNDAY **1985 Story** VS.

A MONOTHEISTICAL POINT OF VIEW!

"FOR GOD, CREATED THE UP AND <u>ADAM</u>
APE STRUCTRED MAN, THAT WE <u>EVE</u> –
VOLVED *from* **controversy."** PAGE 36.

GOSPEL FICTIONS
REFORM TAKES SHAPE
A Straight Look at Questions That Linger,

NO EXPIRATION DATE

CHURCH,

EXPRESSES FEAR OF

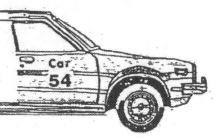

GOD

'TELL IT LIKE IT IS'

'ONLY GOODNESS COMES FROM GOD'•

teaching **Kids** about

GOD

is my BEST FRIEND

AND SIDE KICK; THATS WHY I'M PSYCHIC,

SOUL "SELL" DUMB

AM I LONELY... **Who am I**

I'M THA GANGSTER OF LOVE, OR JUST

ANOTHER KIND OF PAGE 37, PRIEST HOOD .,

'CAUSE I KNOW HOW TO STEAL YOUR HEART HONESTLY!

Who am I

On record

▼

What's Up Doc?

I AM EURE, AND EURE ARE ME!

AND EURE ARE ME, AND I AM EURE.

READING REVOLUTION *Nobody beats him in* **Storytelling.** Own A Moment In Time

BASED ON A ANCIENT BIBLICAL, BELIEF SYSTEM THAT G—OD TOLD ABRAHAM, TO TAKE THA LIFE OF ABE'S SON IN A RITUAL SACRIFICE.—THEN REVENEGED! READING BETWEEN THA LINES IN REALITY IS AN UNEXPLAINED DUEL SPIRITUAL CONFRONTATION THAT WENT ON. ✳ GOD, THE POSITIVE SPIRIT, THE HOLY SPIRIT, WOULD NEVER MINDFULLY SUGGEST TO ANYONE, THIS KIND OF NEGATIVE DELUSIONAL BEHAVIOR, IN THA FIRST PLACE. IN RETROSPECT THIS WEAK-MINDED DEFENDANT WAS DANCING TO THA INVASION OF A NEGATIVE SUGGESTIVE THOUGHT CONCEPT., OR IF YOU WILL' **godzilla** THA BEAST IN **man.** ♫ AMERICA, AMERICA, GOD SHED ~~HIS~~ THY GRACE ON ME!!! PAGE 38.

according to
Slow cooker al pastor

new world WHAT IS PRAYER ACCORDING TO THIS AUTHOR'S RELIGION?

EVERYTHING IN LIFE IS TO A DEGREE; IF YOU ARE PATIENT, YOU CAN MODIFY YOUR OWN BEHAVIOR. THE MAJORITY OF MY PRAYER IS IN MY PERSONALITY AND DECISION MAKINGS, IT'S JUST ONE PLAY AFTER ANOTHER --- BECAUSE TO A GOOD DEGREE I'VE ALWAYS KEPT THE VILLAIN IN ME AS MY UNDERSTUDY... HOW RELIGIOUS AM I? BEING THE MONK AMONG YA, I FIND MYSELF PRAYING TO GOD, FOR GUIDANCE ALL THE TIME! --- IN-FACT THE ONLY TIME I EVER GET LONELY IS WHEN I HAVE TO GO TO THE BATHROOM...

NOTICE TO THE PUBLIC

1982, 'MY RESPONSE TO SHAKESPEARE. YES! "THE WORLD IS A STAGE" - AND OR IN MY WORDS LIFE IS NOTHING BUT A 'PLAY' ON WORDS, OR A WORLDS! IT'S ALL KIND OF LIKE ONE BIG PERSONAL REAL LIFE MOVIE GOING ON OUT THERE; AND I HAVE TO ADMIT FROM TIME TO TIME - I SLEPT THRU IT. ☺

IN READING THIS GRASSROOTS <u>MANUSCRIPT</u> <u>ON ALL (RELIGIOUSLY EDITED PAGES)</u> OF THIS <u>HERE</u> BOOK! THIS WORD "THE" IS ALWAYS IN DIRECT, OR INDIRECT REFERENCE TO GOD. THIS WORD "THA" IS ALWAYS IN DIRECT, OR INDIRECT REFERENCE TO MAN.

"unforgettable images"
'Exorcism' is fascinating !

QUESTION: WHAT'S 'YOUR RELIGIOUS DEPOSITION IN REGARDS TO EXORCISM? "WE SPECIALIZE IN USING A HAND HELD 'DIRT DEVIL' VACUUM CLEANER TO SUCK THE DEVIL RIGHT OUT OF THE OMINOUS; ALONG WITH THE 'INXS' SONG PLAYING IN THE BACKGROUND = ♫ EVERYONE THE DEVIL INSIDE! 'PROCEDURE ENDURES TILL THE ONE THAT'S IN A PREDOMINATE DEMONIAC TRANCE' UTTERS THE TRANS-ITIONAL WORD 'CHIQUITO'! THEREFORE, REGENERATING ONE BACK TO NORMALITY... ☺

When show Business Met Dr. Sunday

Interview factory original

(Transmission in Prayer)

Question: DO I BELIEVE IN MIRACLES?

His Story ANSWER: WELL, SORT OF!

"I COULD NEVER REMEMBER HIS NAME BUT; THERE ONCE WAS THIS BALD HEADED GUY I KNEW, WITH A SEVERE CASE OF CRIPPLING ARTHRITIS; AND HE ASKED ME TO PRAY FOR HIM. (SO I DID!) AND HE ENDED UP WITH A FULL HEAD OF HAIR".

A teachable moment! **First Things First:** PROTESTERS

"ANARCHIES FINEST HOUR"

LIVING IN A SOCIETY WHERE THE BEST WAY TO GET BACK AT AND UN-EMPLOY ALL THOSE RUTHLESS POLICE OFFICERS, ALONG WITH ALL THE HIGHFALUTIN' PEOPLE WORKING IN THE COURT SYSTEM, IS TO 'B-E-H-A-V-E = Y-O-U-R-S-E-L-F' AND THAT'LL HURT'EM OHO SO BIG TIME IN THEIR POCKET BOOKS; ARE YOU G-A-M-E EVERYONE???

America's Most Wanted: 40 PAGE.

((('PRAYER OF THA AFTER THA FACT SOCIETY')))

Vintage Journalism

Discover a New Dimension in Learning

IN TESTIMONY WHEREOF

GOD,

DIDN'T PUT US ON THIS HERE EARTH TO KILL ONE ANOTHER.
STATE OF MIND, FRAME OF MIND,
`NO STATE OF MIND IS PERMANENT!!!

STANDARDIZING OF ONE'S INTELLIGENCE!.

INSTIGATORS OF CRIME **If you ignore `it,`— it will go away.,**

"WHEREAS PATIENCE IS THA KEY!"

Lecturing FEATURES Take My Advice, Please.

AN AFTER SCHOOL SPECIAL MADE TO ORDER.

HAPPY NEW YEAR, 365:
—BARSTOOL SPECTACULAR

Puts You in tha Driver's Seat!

A LITTLE DAB WILL DO YA, IS A HIGHER FORM OF
INTELLIGENCE. PROJECTING MIND OVER MATTER, AS OPPOSE TO
INTOXICATING MATTER OVER MIND! BREAKING IT TO THEM GENTLY
DEVIL IN THA DETAILS— NOWHERE TO HIDE.

FALLING PREY TO LETTING YOUR SHOULDER DEVIL TAKE THA WHEEL,
CAN RESULT INTO SOME HORRIFYING CIRCUMSTANCES. EXCESSIVE USE OF
ALCOHOL WHILE DRIVING IS LIKE A IMPAIRED DEATH DEFYING (SELF-
CENTERED-SIN-DROME!) 'SHOULDER DEVIL' CARD HOLDERS CLUB 'SHOWCASE
EXPOSURE' ANSWERS TO WHAT'S REALLY HAPPENING BEHIND THESE
TRAGIC SCENES. An exclusive book excerpt INSTILLING RESPONSIBILITY.

WHEREAS TRUE 'POSITIVE MORAL MENTORING CAN RESULT IN
BECOMING THE PRECISIAN DRUG, ONE NEVER COMES DOWN FROM"...
"GUIDANCE FROM ABOVE"

book of love 𝄞 ' Setting *Tha Agenda*

1984 **IM PRUV ALL** Seminar

Morals in a biblical tabloid

READINGS FOR REASONING

'THE gospel According to Word Perfect

'All You Need Is a Match' PAGE 41.

"THA REALITY OF TRUE LOVE IS BUILT ON
A POSITIVE (IHONEST)) FOUNDATION."

IN ANY AMELIORATIVE SITUATION,
REFLECTIVELY FOR WHAT IS TRUTH—UNLESS
TWO PARTYS CAN AGREE UPON, YET APPLY TOO.

... And They Lived Happily Ever After

LOVE ⓔⒹucation IS TRUE LOVES gain
AND WINNERS OF A positive FOUNDATION gate.

JORGE PILLER ASSAULT RELATIONSHIP IN A
BEAST ROW GARDEN OF YE DONE.

Lead us not into Shalt Nots,
blame begins.

UNCIVILIZED ABNORMALITY GAMES
ARE THA CAUSE OF SOCIAL INFORMALITYS.

BREAKTHROUGH TRAINING

'MY FAVORITE Position
WITH A WOMAN IS WHEN I ⟶

STOP WONDERING. In This Fine Romance
What Makes Love Last? In Memory of
GOOD OLD-FASHIONED (Affection).

"WHAT'S MORE IMPORTANT THAN SEX IN PAGE 42. A <u>MARITAL</u> RELATIONSHIP? ANSWERS TO LONG HAUL AFFECTION SUPPORT, REASURRANCE!"

foresight Better Homes & Gardens.

'Two Can Play This Game, from tha book of love'.

→ STARTS WITH A HONORABLE MATCH, NOT A HONORABLE MENTION, BUT TO MENTION A CALCULATED OVERALL COMPATIBILITY PURSUIT GAME OF CONSIDERATION, TOWARD A BALANCED FLOW OF HONEST CIRCUMSTANTIAL TRUTH., DANCING TO THA BEAT OF THE RIGHT DRUMMER IS THA RIGHT BASIS OF A POSITIVE RELATIONSHIP, OR LOVE BOAT WITHOUT SINKING. INTIMATE LOVE IS NEVER TAKING ADVANTAGE OF THA ONE YOUR INTOMATE WITH, OR SEPERATION OF OWNERSHIP IS DOING FOR SOMEONE, NOT TO SOMEONE., FOR WHAT IS LESS, IS LESS THAN A HONORABLE Education.

As I see this **Romance Is Here To Stay** ◉ (QUESTIONS OF <u>THA HEART</u>) YOU Know

IT'S TIME TO START THINKING THAT THERE'S OTHER FISH IN THA SEA, WHEN INSTEAD OF FEELING THA PAIN OF ⇒ — CUPID'S ARROWS → YOUR ACTUALLY BEING HARPOONED.

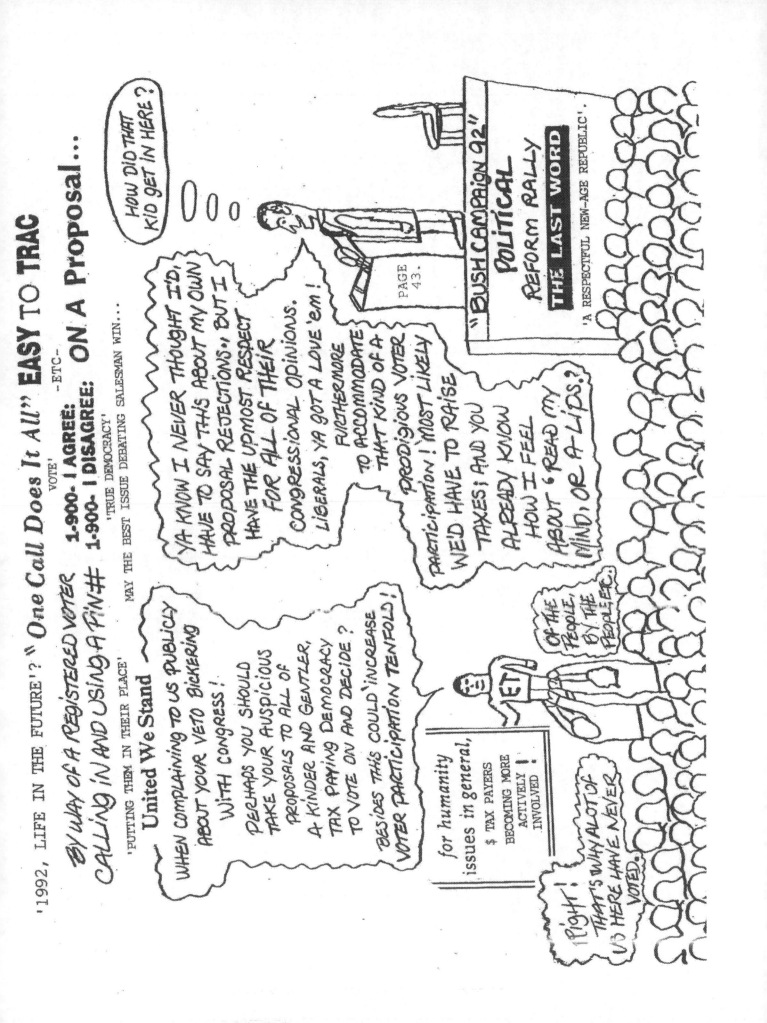

A PROMISE FULFILLED

DELIVERS.

redefining our politics.

YOU ARE HERE

Vintage Journalism

The Wait Is Over.

Reality Check Be Prepared To Be Impressed.

"read this book!"

AND

God Let Us Find Him

Blessed to live in Reno

HISTORY WILL BE STAGED.

STEP BY STEP, *A Whole New*

Constitutional freedom *Phenomenon.*

"A Hidden World Discovery Kit

For THIS Voice of the Voiceless, *is*

The `Real Day The Earth Stood Still ...

Author Biography
A biography of tha writer of that book. So please let us know a little about you. where you live, and other pertinent highlights about your interests:

1988
RENO NEVADA: THA TRIALS AND TRIBULATIONS OF GOING ABOUT AND BEING AN UNRECOGNIZABLE SUPERSTAR LIVING IN A ONE HORSE TOWN AND LOVING EVERY MINUTE OF IT.

This is the end.

TODAY I MUST CONFESS

After Tha Fall

"WE COULD BE IN STORE FOR SOMEWHAT OF A MILD WINTER! :)

Without TRUTH our world could not go on.

A way into the system
aims to 'revitalize' society

miracle on **45** *th* page ARE WE THERE YET?

Your Audience Needs to Know!

Happenings Around Town

People in Support.
Tha Beginning:

SIGNED official :

A B C'er of ROBOT SCHOOL.

ARE PEOPLE TREATING YOU LIKE AN ALIEN?

"IN THIS MAN'S RELIGION THERE'S GOD IN MAN,
BUT THERE'S NO SUCH THING AS A MAN THAT'S GOD!"

THE GOSPEL ACCORDING TO A CONCLUSION!

YOUR GUIDE TO *The `Real Day The Earth Stood Still* (((COUNTDOWN)))
'Warning' to Russian, or Martian and celebrate a structured man is a
'dooms day scenario.' Whereas there's only one God, reeling in the diving light line,
out of sight 'positive' SPIRIT in the sky...

Printed in the United States
By Bookmasters